P r a i s e   f o r

DOING CHURCH AS A TEAM

Doing Church as a Team is one of the most refreshing books I have read in a long time. I have made it mandatory reading for all of my pastoral staff.

Ché Ahn
SENIOR PASTOR, HARVEST ROCK CHURCH
PASADENA, CALIFORNIA

Every time I talk to Wayne Cordeiro, I am inspired and enthused about what God is doing through his church in Hawaii. *Doing Church as a Team* is easy to understand and easy to apply. Every church leader should read this book.

Bob Buford
FOUNDING CHAIRMAN, LEADERSHIP NETWORK

Wayne Cordeiro is one of the spiritual giants of our time. No better book exists on the subject of building teams.

Bill Easum
EASUM, BANDY AND ASSOCIATES

Very few young leaders at the dawn of this new millennium have Wayne Cordeiro's combination of gifts, character and leadership. I am completely unreserved in recommending his work because I know him well. I trust his vision and values in both a personal and public dimension, and I believe he is being raised up by God as a voice to the larger Body at this pivotal time in the Church.

Jack W. Hayford
FOUNDING PASTOR, THE CHURCH ON THE WAY
CHANCELLOR, THE KING'S COLLEGE AND SEMINARY
VAN NUYS, CALIFORNIA

By definition, leaders build teams, and Wayne Cordeiro is one of the best team-building leaders I've ever known. I suggest you visit New Hope Fellowship in Hawaii and witness firsthand just how thrilling ministry can be when the right people are serving in the right places, shoulder to shoulder with others who love serving Christ together. Read this book slowly and absorb its contents fully. You will discover there is no limit to what God can do through a church that does its ministry as a team.

Bill Hybels
SENIOR PASTOR, WILLOW CREEK COMMUNITY CHURCH
SOUTH BARRINGTON, ILLINOIS

A joyous book written in the breezy style of a native island song, *Doing Church as a Team* isn't just about mobilizing people to do the work of the church. This is about releasing people into a whole new spiritual dimension in their lives—a place where they begin to understand that God created each of us for a purpose. Mahalo, Wayne!

John C. Maxwell
FOUNDER, THE INJOY GROUP

Wayne Cordeiro's thriving congregation is one of America's truly great churches. *Doing Church as a Team*, however, is not about how to build a megachurch. Wayne is committed to building people one by one. His passion is to help every believer find his or her unique place of fruitful service in God's house and among the lost in God's harvest fields.

Ron Mehl
FORMER PASTOR, BEAVERTON FOURSQUARE CHURCH
BEAVERTON, OREGON

The key word in this book is "team." Wayne Cordeiro is equipping people for leadership and giving them a vision of how to pull together to build the work of God. The principles in this book will work in a church of fifty as well as they do in Pastor Cordeiro's megachurch in Honolulu.

Elmer L. Towns
DEAN OF THE SCHOOL OF RELIGION, LIBERTY UNIVERSITY

There is no such thing as a formula for growing a church, but there are foundational principles underlying the growth of every one. Wayne Cordeiro has these principles in place, and he shares his secrets in this remarkable book.

C. Peter Wagner
CHANCELLOR, WAGNER LEADERSHIP INSTITUTE

DOING CHURCH *as a* TEAM

WAYNE CORDEIRO

Regal

From Gospel Light
Ventura, California, U.S.A.

PUBLISHED BY REGAL BOOKS
FROM GOSPEL LIGHT
VENTURA, CALIFORNIA, U.S.A.
Regal PRINTED IN THE U.S.A.

Regal Books is a ministry of Gospel Light, a Christian publisher dedicated to serving the local church. We believe God's vision for Gospel Light is to provide church leaders with biblical, user-friendly materials that will help them evangelize, disciple and minister to children, youth and families.

It is our prayer that this Regal book will help you discover biblical truth for your own life and help you meet the needs of others. May God richly bless you.

For a free catalog of resources from Regal Books/Gospel Light, please call your Christian supplier or contact us at 1-800-4-GOSPEL *or* www.regalbooks.com.

2004 revised and expanded edition

© 2001, 2004 by Wayne Cordeiro
All rights reserved.

Cover design by David Griffing

Library of Congress Cataloging-in-Publication Data
Cordeiro, Wayne.
    Doing church as a team / Wayne Cordeiro.—Rev. and expanded ed.
        p. cm.
    Includes bibliographical references.
    ISBN 978-0-8307-3681-2
    1. Church work. I. Title.
    BV4400.C66 2005
    253—dc22   2004026661

Rights for publishing this book in other languages are contracted by Gospel Light Worldwide, the international nonprofit ministry of Gospel Light. Gospel Light Worldwide also provides publishing and technical assistance to international publishers dedicated to producing Sunday School and Vacation Bible School curricula and books in the languages of the world. For additional information, visit www.gospellightworldwide.org; write to Gospel Light Worldwide, P.O. Box 3875, Ventura, CA 93006; or send an e-mail to info@gospellightworldwide.org.

CONTENTS

ACKNOWLEDGMENTS

No one stands alone. In my life, dozens of people have given me input and inspiration for this book. I have been mentored by scores of wonderful people who may never win a prize or get their names in print. These are my silent heroes—men and women who have jewel-studded crowns awaiting them from the One they so willingly serve.

Thank you, wonderful New Hope family of churches all over the world. We have chosen to live life together as colaborers. You are my family. To the hundreds of volunteers who put their hands to the plow and have never looked back, thank you.

Thank you, my publishing partners at Regal, who have been so supportive in all my endeavors.

Great gratitude and love also go to my dear wife, Anna, and my children, Amy, Aaron and Abigail, from whom I have learned so much. I have so much yet to learn, but with your love and support, I will never give up! Each one of you is a gift to my life.

I have no greater joy than to team up with thousands of churches as together we make a difference. The *Life Journals* bring us closer to our Master, and *Doing Church as a Team* will bring us closer to our calling as saints on this spinning globe.

A PRAYER ANSWERED?

I have often wrestled with the fact that if the Word of God indeed is powerful, then why does the average church in America have fewer than 100 people in attendance every Sunday morning? Also, though violent crime has declined in many places, the prison population in America has dramatically risen by 500 percent since 1975.[1] With more than 300,000 churches in the United States, why haven't we done better?

I know we can.

I believe that if we join hearts and hands and learn from each other, we can bring this country back from the brink. But we have to work together.

Rick Warren, pastor of Saddleback Community Church in Southern California, once quipped, "I offered a man an idea to try, but he declined and told me in no uncertain terms that he was going to either be original or nothing . . . so he became both."

My dear friend Tom Paterson described it like this, with a gleam in his eye: "If I have one good idea, and you have one good idea, how many ideas does each of us have? One. Now, if I share my idea with you and you share yours with me, how many does each one now have? *Two!* You see, if we share our ideas with each other, we have immediately doubled our knowledge. Have you lost your own idea? No! You still have it. But by sharing ideas, we have increased our knowledge 100 percent."

You never dim the light of your own candle by lighting that of another.

I often pray that we will always remain learners. The Greek word for "disciple" (*mathetes*), in fact, comes from the verb *manthano*, "to learn." Humility and teachability are the crown jewels of all the qualities of a leader whom God will use in the twenty-first century. When we stop learning, we just stop.

Jigoro Kano understood this. He founded the art of judo and became the highest-ranking black belt in this world-renowned sport. Nearing his death, Kano made one last request of his students. He asked that they bury him wearing a white belt, the symbol of a beginner, a learner.

May we learn God's design for His people and begin to respect and appreciate each other's giftings!

I for one am learning that I cannot be fulfilled apart from other people. In fact, the bottom line of this book is this: *You can't do it alone.* If you want to be a successful leader—if you plan to have a successful ministry—then you must develop not only your gifts but also the gifts of those around you. If you give your life away, you'll end up discovering what life is all about.

The ideas in *Doing Church as a Team* are more than just the accumulation of 30 years in ministry. I have included lessons learned from making hundreds of mistakes as well as gems gleaned from observing many wonderful churches and leaders in action.

This book is written for both pastors and members of congregations who have a deep desire to make a difference with their lives. I pray you'll come away motivated and inspired in your walk with the Lord, encouraged to keep reaching for God's very best. It is written for leaders who, like myself, have found the status quo unacceptable. At times I will address my comments to pastors and, at other times, to volunteer leaders. But in the final analysis, these truths apply to every person and every church in every denomination.

Finally, this isn't a book on how to make your church more like our church, or how to adopt another congregation's style. Instead, it is a book on how to become more like the person or church Jesus created *you* to be. We must learn from each other, and if we do, we'll be miles closer to becoming all God desires for us.

Just before Jesus' arrest and crucifixion, He prayed a remarkable prayer for the church He founded. He asked His Father, "that they may all be one; even as Thou, Father, art in Me, and I in Thee, that they also may be in Us; that the world may believe that Thou didst send Me" (John 17:21, *KJV*).

I often notice that, as Christians, we constantly ask God to answer our prayers. There's nothing inherently wrong with that; He invites our prayers and is so faithful to answer them. But after reading this verse, I thought, *Wouldn't it be nice if, just for once, we could answer one of HIS prayers?*

Doing church as a team is one of the ways we can do that. That's what this book is all about. After all, He has answered hundreds of billions of our prayers. Now maybe we can finally answer one of His.

Note

1. Charles Colson, "Not Out of the Woods: Why Crime Is Falling," *BreakPoint with Chuck Colson*, broadcast February 10, 1999. Transcript is available on the Internet at http://www.breakpoint.org.

REACHING FOR GOD'S BEST

*This is what the LORD says—your Redeemer, the Holy One of Israel:
"I am the LORD your God, who teaches you what is best for you, who
directs you in the way you should go."*

ISAIAH 48:17, *NIV*

Nestled between the two mountains of Mauna Kea and Mauna
Loa, Hilo is one of the most beautiful cities in the Hawaiian
Islands. Eastward lies a natural bay that welcomed some of the
first missionaries to Hawaii. Located at the foot of these two
imposing mountains, Hilo receives constant rain showers, giving
it title to the wettest city in the United States, with an average
annual rainfall of more than 120 inches.

Hilo also has some of the most beautiful people in the
world. They are fun-loving, relationship-oriented men and
women with much *aloha*, or love, for one another. They enjoy

sports, fishing, eating, music and laughter.

One of the more popular sports on the islands is canoe paddling. In this sport, six paddlers make up the engine room for an outrigger canoe of the type that traversed the islands more than 200 years ago. Although navigating one of these ancient canoes may look like child's play, the actual technique requires much more than meets the eye.

One summer, six of us from the church received an invitation to compete as a crew in an upcoming canoe race. We were game for something new, so we accepted the invitation and immediately sought out a canoe instructor from a nearby club. We started our first lesson in a lake of brackish water. Our instructor sat astride the nose of the canoe, facing us as he called out signals and instructions. Once we took our places, the first lesson began.

"OK, everyone!" he yelled. "This is how you hold a paddle." Then he modeled the correct form. As we figured out which end we were supposed to grasp, and with which hand, he continued to instruct us.

"We're going to paddle our first stretch of water. It will be an eighth-of-a-mile sprint. When I begin the stopwatch and say 'Go!' just paddle as fast and as hard as you can. When we cross the finish line, I'll notify you. That's when you can stop paddling. Got it?"

How hard can this be? I thought. *Even children paddle canoes. This ought to be a breeze!* Just then, the sharp call of our coach shattered my self-confident thoughts.

"*Ho`omakaukau?I mua!*"

In English, that means, "Ready? Go forward!"

With our muscles bulging and sinews stretched, we burst out of our dead-in-the-water starting position like a drowning elephant trying to get air. We thrashed the water with our paddles on either side of the canoe. Not knowing when to switch from one side to the other, we all figured it made sense to switch when one arm got tired. So, firing at will, I crossed the blade of my oar over and across the canoe; and when I did, I scraped the back of my fellow paddler seated directly in front of me. He grunted as my oar etched a red mark across his spine. But neither of us stopped. We just kept wildly flailing our arms like amateur ice skaters trying to regain their balance. We were on a crusade!

Yet soon it felt as if hours had elapsed. My arms began to feel heavy as lead and my lungs felt on fire. My teammate's back had started to bleed, and water had filled our canoe halfway to the top. The elephant was beginning to drown when we finally heard our coach say, "OK, stop!"

Thank God! I thought. We abandoned the sinking canoe and let our bodies slump into the water, totally exhausted.

"One minute, forty-two seconds," our coach called out. "Pretty sad!"

Like war-torn warriors, we comforted each other, apologizing for the scrapes and wounds inflicted by our flailing paddles. We started bailing water out of the lumbering canoe, which by now looked more like a listing submarine than a sleek racing vessel.

Coach gathered us whimpering novices together and, after sharing a few basics about safety, taught us how to paddle as a team. Each fledgling paddler was to mirror the man in front of him, and everyone was to move in time with the lead stroker. Coach taught us how to switch our paddles to the opposite hand without injuring each other. We practiced together again and again until our stroking became as rhythmic as a metronome. We were beginning to look good! After a few practice runs, Coach took us back to our original starting position.

"All right," he said, "let's try that same eighth-mile stretch again! Only this time, I want you to stroke as if you were taking a leisurely stroll through the park. No sprinting. Just mirror the one in front of you and switch with a smooth cadence of rhythm, just as you were taught. Stroke as a team. Feel the movement of the canoe. It's sort of like riding a skateboard. Once you get it going, you just nurse the glide. And don't try to break any sound barriers this time, OK?"

With new confidence, we took our mark. Coach barked out the starting signal.

"*Ho`omakaukau? I mua!*"

Our oars silently entered the water, coordinated in perfect time. Our canoe cut through the water like a knife through jelly. We switched sides without skipping a beat. We each mirrored the rower in front of us. Somehow, in just a few minutes, we had been transformed from a drowning circus animal into a precision machine! Then, just as we began to feel the exhilaration of our smooth progress, our jubilant coach yelled, "OK! Stop paddling!"

This ahead-of-expected arrival caught all of us by surprise.

"Anybody tired?"

We all shook our heads no.

Coach held up his stopwatch so that we could see the truth. Then he exclaimed, "You beat your last time by twenty-four seconds!"

We couldn't believe it. Nobody injured? No one overboard? No one exhausted enough to keel over? No canoe deluged with water? No fire in my lungs?

In sheer delight, we congratulated each other, gave a few victory shouts, exchanged leis and took pictures. This was amazing!

And we did it *together*. We had paddled as a team.

As Old As the Bible

Doing church as a team is not an innovative concept. In fact, it is as old as the Bible itself (but I hope to describe teamwork in more contemporary terms).

This approach to "doing church" lies at the very heart and passion of an amazing church in Honolulu called New Hope Christian Fellowship of Oahu—our tenth pioneer work since 1984. Within nine years of establishment, the congregation's average attendance on Sunday mornings has risen to 10,500. More than 26,000 people have made first-time commitments to follow Christ, and more than 4,000 of those people have been baptized.

The church outgrew me in its first month. If it weren't for the outstanding servants whom God brought there to serve, I am sure I would have been locked away in the mental ward of a state institution by now (perhaps some people feel I should be admitted anyway!). Because of our accelerated growth, doing church as a team was almost a necessity.

I think I saw it all come together for the first time at a 1996 Christmas Eve service. We put on a program filled with multimedia presentations, dance, mime, drama, a 100-voice choir with smaller ensembles—I mean, the works. The auditorium filled up with more than 1,200 people, many of whom had come for the very first time. I stood just offstage, watching the evening unfold.

During the prior year, our first year in Oahu, we had seen more than 1,400 people open their hearts to Christ. Whenever you gather so many new believers in one place, you will have fire! The evening's music erupted with a song of magnificent celebration. Dancers burst onto the stage, expressing their exuberance with cartwheels and twists. A former university cheerleader came bounding across the platform with flips and somersaults. Others got tossed into the air for the finale, and the auditorium broke into applause. (One girl flew so high, we haven't heard from her since!)

Sometime during this program, it hit me. As I watched our outstanding keyboardist play the piano with all his heart, I thought, *He is preaching the gospel the best way he knows how—through his piano!*

Nearby, the drummer played the drums with his usual excellence. He seemed to be playing more with his heart than with drumsticks. That night I said to myself, *Our drummer is preaching the gospel the best way he knows how—through his drums!*

When I looked into the radiant faces of the choir, I saw many lives that had been recently transformed by the Lord's grace, and I thought, *Those wonderful people are all preaching the gospel the best way they know how—through their singing!*

> *Few things are more beautiful to God than seeing His people serve and work together in a united rhythm. It's like a symphony to His ears.*

The mime, the drama team and the ensemble all preached the gospel through their own gifts.

Then I noticed the stage coordinators moving with poise and rhythm, rearranging microphones and straightening cords. I saw our video people running the cameras. I looked out over the audience and observed the ushers greeting people with genuine enthusiasm. I spotted the faces of various individuals who had brought along friends and neighbors. All these people were preaching the gospel through their particular gifts, passions and talents.

At the end of a memorable program, I walked out onto the platform, picked up a microphone and wrapped up the evening with a simple presentation of the gospel. I, too, preached the gospel the best way I knew how, through my own gift. But I wasn't doing it alone. We were all doing it together! We were all preaching the gospel the best way we knew how—through our gifts. And that included the children's workers, the parking lot team and everyone who had worked behind the scenes to make this evening happen. Every single person had a part. I saw this event not merely as one presentation of the gospel but as several hundred presentations of the gospel—all at the same time in one evening. That's what made it so powerful!

That night I started to see the truth clearly, and a brand-new understanding of how beautiful the Body of Christ can be flooded my soul.

We were starting to do church as a team!

Although I had been in ministry for more than two decades, this experience made me more certain than ever that I knew much less than I thought I did. Yet through all of our trials and struggles, God formed a diamond and fashioned a gem.

Today, my heart's desire is to deposit the truths I have learned in Hawaii into your account.

Designed for Each Other

God would never have given us the Great Commission—to go into all the world and preach the gospel—if He never had intended for us to actually move forward. Peter tells us that the Lord is not willing "for any to perish but for all to come to repentance" (2 Pet. 3:9). God would not say such a thing if it were not possible.

We are all called into this great work, but none of us can do it alone. No pastor can single-handedly fulfill such a calling, regardless of how gifted he may be. Unless every one of us catches the fire, in the long run we will lack any warmth against the chill of this present age.

Few things are more beautiful to God than seeing His people serve and work together in a united rhythm. It's like a symphony to His ears. That's how we were created to function. God designed us to need each other. To reach our communities, much less the world, we need every ministry doing its part and every congregation excitedly doing church as a team.

Stroking Together for a Purpose

Just like paddling a canoe, God designed His people to stroke together for a purpose. He has designed each church with a special purpose, and He plans to saturate the carrying out of that purpose with joy. In order for this to happen, God has given each of us a unique gift. The combination of our gifts working in sync should give off such a joyful radiance that the whole world stands up and takes notice.

God has given each of us a paddle—a gift, a calling. And like the paddlers in a canoe, each of us has a vital place to serve or a unique role to fill. On each paddle is our unique thumbprint, our own individual circuitry, designed by God Himself. He places each of us in a community—more specifically, a local church—with a divine purpose. He fits us alongside others with a similar assignment and calls us a family, a team, the Church. No one person is called to carry out this assignment alone; God didn't design it that way. He created us to do church as a team!

A full symphony under the direction of a master conductor will always sound infinitely better than a one-man band. As we discover and develop our individual gifts and learn to stroke in rhythm as a team, we will be astonished at how much further and faster we go—and with far fewer injuries!

Now, continue with me on an adventure that can transform churches. It will renovate your thinking like it did mine.

"*Ho`omakaukau? I mua!*" (Ready? Let's go forward!)

Team Preparation

1. What seems more similar to your experience of church, Wayne's first try at paddling the canoe, or his second? Why?

2. What does the phrase, "doing church as a team," mean to you right now? What images come to mind?

3. Read Matthew 28:18-20 and 2 Peter 3:9. What do these verses suggest to you about the mission of your church? What do they suggest about doing church as a team?

GOD HAS A PLAN

*You did not choose Me, but I chose you, and appointed you, that you
should go and bear fruit, and that your fruit should remain.*

JOHN 15:16

God doesn't do things at random. He has a plan, both for you
and for your church.

God planned your birth before you were even conceived, just
as He did the prophet Jeremiah's (see Jer. 1:5). He chose you, created you and then delicately placed you on His sovereign time
continuum.

God never makes mistakes. I have searched the Bible thorough-
ly, and I have yet to find even one instance when God said, "Oops!"

If God had wanted to, He could have caused you to be born
at another time. You could have been born in any of the years
before Christ. But for some reason, He wanted you to be born

and to live now, in this century, in this day and age. He also could have programmed it so that you'd be living in a nation other than the one you currently call home. But He didn't. Why? *He has a plan.*

Of all the states in the United States of America, He has chosen for me to live in a tiny grouping of islands called Hawaii (thank God!). To many people, the islands don't seem very prestigious. Ever try locating Hawaii on a globe? Too quick of a spin and the whole archipelago disappears. You have a better chance of finding Hawaii with a map. But then again, such a strategy may confuse you just as much. For many years, I thought Hawaii was located just off the tip of Alaska. Why? Because on every map I ever saw while growing up, Hawaii appeared in a small box located just off the Alaskan coastline!

God preselected the city where you live. He even placed you in the very neighborhood where you now reside. Furthermore, of all the churches He could have put you in, He has placed you in one specific church.

I think that's a miracle! It took a great deal of planning on God's part—something the Bible tells us He's *very* good at:

> From one man he made every nation of men, that they should inhabit the whole earth; and he determined the times set for them and the exact places where they should live (Acts 17:26, *NIV*).

God determined the exact places where we should live and He decided the precise generation into which we would be born. The Bible says, "For we are His workmanship, created in Christ Jesus for good works, which God prepared beforehand, that we should walk in them" (Eph. 2:10). God prepared our paths beforehand and He has a plan for each of us. And now it is our responsibility to find out what that plan is so we can walk in it.

God chose you for a very specific purpose, and if God didn't have expectations for you to succeed in that purpose, He wouldn't have allowed you to be born. He never would have bothered to create you. You have only one life to live for Christ on Earth. Invest it wisely!

Life Beyond the Scratch

This globe we're riding on is not as still as it may appear. It's actually traveling at more than 6,600 miles per hour. Think of it! Earth is rotating faster than the spin cycle of your washing machine. No wonder the psalmist declares life to be as transient as a "breath" (Ps. 144:4), the passing of our years but a "sigh" (Ps. 90:9). James likens our life to a "vapor," here today and gone tomorrow (Jas. 4:14). Our life indeed flashes before our eyes. A few more spins and it will be over; we'll all be in eternity.

How long is eternity? Imagine a cable that extends in both directions till it disappears over opposite horizons. It passes through both walls on either side of the room you're sitting in and stretches unseen into the distance. That's eternity—it goes on forever, with no end in sight.

Now compare eternity to the length of your life on Earth. In your imagination, take out a ballpoint pen and draw a vertical scratch on the infinite cable stretched out in front of you. The width of that mark (about ½₂ of an inch) represents the length of our life on Earth, compared with eternity. Not very long!

The trouble is, most people think that all they have is that little scratch. So they hold on to it, caress it, love it. They save and hoard for that scratch. They live scratch lives, have scratch businesses, raise scratch families with scratch hopes and scratch dreams. But they're doomed, because that scratch will soon come to an end.

Yet God in His grace gives us hope. Listen to my interpretation of John 3:16. It's sort of the revised *slandered* version, but it makes the point: "God so loved the *scratch* that He sent His only begotten Son, that whosoever would believe in Him would not perish *on that scratch* but have eternal life."

Millions today still don't know that life exists beyond the scratch. They end up trying to hang on to the scratch, wondering, *Is this all there is?*

Even in the midst of their futile efforts and raw confusion, they know deep inside that there *has* to be something more. And there is! The Bible says that God put eternity in the heart of everyone (see Eccles. 3:11). This is why each person longs for more than what the world can offer. Seventeenth-century French philosopher and humble Christian, Blaise Pascal, once said there is a God-shaped void in the heart of everyone. Although many try to fill this void with the world's varied and widely available substitutes, that aching chasm can be filled only with God Himself.

The fact that you are reading this book is a good sign that you have allowed God to fill your heart. What an amazing grace He has extended to you and me! But that's not all there is. Let me tell you the rest of the story.

God's Reason for Saving Us

Salvation is not simply divine life insurance, nor is it the Christian's "fire escape." If getting you to heaven were the only reason God saved you, then the moment you received Christ, God would have killed you. Why keep you around? His job would have been complete. He might as well get you onward and upward to heaven. There would be no use for you hanging around here just taking up space.

But heaven wasn't the only reason God saved you. Salvation includes you, but it's not all about you. It is what God wants to do *through* you.

Instead of taking you immediately home, God placed a message in your heart—a message of good news about hope beyond the scratch for anyone who "will call upon the name of the LORD" (Rom. 10:13). Then He put you back on that scratch for a few more spins. There's a purpose to your life—a divine plan for you. Soon your life and mine will be over; but until then, we have a message to deliver.

> *Salvation includes you, but it's not all about you. It is what God wants to do* through *you.*

It's easy to get distracted in this world of options. We can live 100 years but still miss life by a mile. I wonder how many of us can keep constantly busy in life without ever completing the assignment for which we were born?

Nice Life, Wrong Assignment

A friend of mine once told me a story that still makes me chuckle. While in college, he approached the end of a term, still needing to complete a major paper in order to graduate. After sleepless nights and many tiresome trips to the library, he completed his paper and turned it in. Three days later, when each student received his or her work back, he found these words from his professor written on the paper (in red): "Good research. Great illustrations. Wonderful bibliography. Grade: 'F' . . . WRONG ASSIGNMENT!"

I still laugh when I think of his story, but it also holds a poignant truth for each of us. I certainly don't want to stand before God on that final day and hear Him say: "Nice house. Great job. Nice boat. Wonderful salary. Grade: 'F' . . . Wrong assignment!"

I imagine the Lord could even give such a grade to churches: "Great building program. Nice socials. Great prayer meetings. Beautiful sanctuary renovation. Grade: 'F' . . . Wrong assignment!"

When we get to heaven, we will see many wonderful things: golden streets, mansions, angels, cherubim and seraphim . . . but let me tell you one thing we will never see again. We will never see another non-Christian. For the rest of eternity, we will never have another opportunity to share the good news with those who do not know Christ. *Now* is the only chance we have to tell others about the hope available to everyone beyond the scratch, to tell the redemptive story that invites people to eternal life.

The Father will ask only one question of us on that day. The question won't be "How large of a salary did you make?" Nor will it be "How popular were you?" He will ask us only one thing: "How many people did you bring with you?"

I dare not answer with such a weak reply as "Lord, You should have seen our choir! Why, it was featured in our denominational magazine last month! Oh, and our new steeple. You could see it for miles!" I can imagine God responding with eyes that would pierce my soul as He said, "Read My lips: *How many did you bring with you?*"

What will we talk about for all of eternity if, when we arrive, we have not been about our Father's business? We have one chance to accomplish what God sent us to accomplish on this scratch. And that's all.

His Plan, Our Responsibility

A Christian nurse attended a very sick man confined to the intensive care unit of a hospital. Although the man was only in his early sixties, death loomed closer with each passing day. The nurse consistently prayed for his healing, but the man's hardened heart only mocked her attempts.

"Don't need to pray for me, I've got no reason to live," his crotchety voice reprimanded her. Yet she persisted. Still, as the days slipped by, so did his chances for recovery. One evening, his breathing became so labored that the doctors feared he wouldn't make it through the night. That evening his nurse spent extra hours by his bedside, talking to him about his soul and praying overtime for his healing.

The following morning, the nurse arrived back at work, expecting to find an empty bed. But instead of an empty bed, to her surprise, she found her patient sitting up, eating breakfast and looking remarkably healthy.

"Praise the Lord!" she exclaimed. "You're healed!"

"Yup!" he cheerfully replied. "I feel great. You and your prayers healed me."

"Oh no, I didn't heal you," the nurse quickly replied. "God did. And now it is your responsibility to find out why."

God has saved us and given each of us a second chance. Now we must find out why. It's time that we paused long enough to recalibrate our direction.

Jesus tells us in Mark 8:36, "For what does it profit a man to gain the whole world, and forfeit his soul?" Most of us can easily point out the application of this saying for someone who does not know Christ. What about its application for us as Christians? For the follower of Christ, it might apply in this way: "What would it profit a Christian if all his prayers were answered—a fine house, abundant income, blessings galore—but he missed the very reason for which God created him?" What a waste that would be!

The application gets no more cheery for a church that loses its way: "What would it profit a church if all its programs thrived—a large student ministry, a dynamic worship experience, an expanding campus—but it missed the very reason for which God had called it into being?" What a colossal waste that would be!

The harvest will not self-reap, but it will self-destruct if not reaped. We must never forget who we are and who we were meant to be on this spinning globe.

Take a few moments and ask yourself why you think God created you. Why did He place you where you are? Think also of your church. Why did He call it into being? Why did He put it where it is?

God makes no mistakes. Both you and your church are on a special assignment during your short stay on Earth.

Team Preparation

1. What would you say is the specific purpose for which God caused you to be born?
2. What do you think God wants to accomplish through you?
3. What is your specific, divine assignment on this "scratch"?
4. Why do you think God placed you where you are? Why did He place your church where it is?

DON'T FORGET WHO YOU ARE

For our citizenship is in heaven.

PHILIPPIANS 3:20

An old story tells of a rabbi living in a Russian city a century ago. Disappointed by his lack of direction and life purpose, he wandered in the chilly evening. With his hands thrust deep in his pockets, he aimlessly walked through the empty streets, questioning his faith in God, the Scriptures and his calling to ministry. The only thing colder than the Russian winter air was the chill within his soul. He felt so enshrouded by his own despair that he mistakenly wandered into a Russian military compound off limits to civilians.

The bark of a Russian soldier shattered the silence of the evening chill. "Who are you? And what are you doing here?"

"Excuse me?" replied the rabbi.

"I said, 'Who are you and what are you doing here?'"

After a brief moment, the rabbi, in a gracious tone so as not to provoke the soldier, said, "How much do you get paid every day?"

"What does that have to do with you?" the soldier retorted.

With the delight of someone making a new discovery, the rabbi said, "I will pay you the equal sum if you will ask me those same two questions every day: 'Who are you?' and 'What are you doing here?'"

Let me be that Russian soldier for you as you read the next few pages. I will ask you those same two questions:

Who are you? What are you doing here?

Just Like the Israelites

The children of Israel suffered a recurring problem of forgetfulness. We see repeatedly in the Old Testament that the Lord often had to remind them of who they were:

Beware lest you forget (Deut. 8:11).

God had sternly warned the Israelites that if they should ever forget Him, they could expect disaster as the only result:

And it shall come about if you ever forget the LORD your God, . . . you shall surely perish. Like the nations that the LORD makes to perish before you, so you shall perish (Deut. 8:19-20).

On the other hand, God promised the Israelites that if they would not forget, then He would give them victory over their enemies and firm control of the new land. If they let their memories slip, however, the opposite would occur. They would surely perish.

God made many similar promises to His people under the Old Covenant. We must understand, however, that a major difference exists between a *covenant* and a *promise*. A covenant may *include* a promise, but that promise often carries requirements to be fulfilled. In the text; this usually shows up as an "if-then" proposition. "*If* you do this, *then* I will do that."

Consider one example of a covenant that includes a promise whose fulfillment depends on our response:

> If my people, which are called by my name, shall humble themselves, and pray, and seek my face, and turn from their wicked ways; then will I hear from heaven, and will forgive their sin, and will heal their land (2 Chron. 7:14, *KJV*).

God will always faithfully do whatever He has promised. Joshua 21:45 reminds us, "Not one of the good promises which the LORD had made to the house of Israel failed; all came to pass." Beyond all question, we can trust His integrity and faithfulness. He will never back out or fail to deliver. He will always remain true to His Word. We love the promises of God, but we sometimes fail to see that we might actually be reading a covenant that *includes* a promise. And that's not exactly the same thing. God certainly will fulfill His promises whether we remember Him or not; but when that promise appears within the zip code of a covenant, we dare not forget!

In the wilderness, God occasionally asked the Israelites to build stone altars as a testimony to some important event. Wherever God performed a miracle of provision or of victory, His people were to build an altar. Ever wonder why? God wanted to remind them of who they were as a people and who they were supposed to be representing. So when their children one day asked, "What do these stones mean?" their fathers were to remind them of God's greatness as they traversed the wilderness for forty years (see Josh. 4:20-24). They simply could not afford to forget.

Forgetting Can Be a Scary Thing

A few summers ago, my son, Aaron, and three of his friends found a 55-gallon barrel and a sloping hill. The combination of these two discoveries by a group of teenage boys could only spell mischief. And so it did. They thought it would be great fun to get inside the barrel and roll down the hill.

Aaron was the first to volunteer his life and future (I think he got his bravery from his mother). The barrel took off on a slow, labored roll with Aaron inside but soon accelerated into an out-of-control, warp-speed, one-man suicide mission. The barrel began flipping end-over-end until it came to a crashing halt at the bottom of the hill. Somewhere along that wild ride, Aaron hit his head on the side of the barrel and got knocked out cold. When he regained consciousness a short time later, he couldn't remember a thing. He had sustained a concussion, resulting in temporary amnesia.

I was at a meeting when I received an anxious call from one of his friends and partners in crime. He reported that Aaron had hit his head and had no recollection of anything that had taken place. I rushed home immediately to find a very frightened sixteen-year-old boy with temporary amnesia. Although Aaron is a virile, strapping young man, I had never seen him so afraid.

"Dad, I can't remember anything!" he said through tears. "I'm so scared!" He couldn't say exactly who he was. With a father's confidence, I reassured him that his erased memory would soon return, probably in a day or two. But despite my best efforts to assure him, Aaron remained anxious and uncertain.

We drove him to the emergency room, where I had the dubious honor of explaining to the attending physicians how this concussion happened. The doctors wheeled him into a room for a CT scan, and about an hour later, the ER physician returned. He informed us that Aaron's memory would return in a day or two and that the scan of his brain came back normal (which, frankly, surprised me. After a stunt like that, it shocked me that they had found any gray matter at all in his cranium. I also thought it might benefit each of his friends to take one of those scans. In fact, I told the technician that I wouldn't be surprised if he found them all empty).

We took Aaron home, and the following day his memory returned to normal. He recuperated quickly from his injury and came away with a little more wisdom about empty barrels, sloping hills and friends willing to nominate each another to boldly go where no one in his right mind has gone before. But I will always remember how frightened my son felt that day when he lost his memory, even though I assured him that it would be temporary. And do you want to know how I had such confidence to diagnose his condition as "temporary" amnesia?

Let's just call it experience. I've volunteered for a few brainless adventures myself.

When the people of Israel forgot who they were, they heard no alarms, saw no flashing lights and made no emergency 9-1-1 calls. With the occasional exception of a lone prophet, no one even noticed that anything had gone very wrong.

Today, however, we have a Helper, the Holy Spirit, who reminds us that God has given us an identity and a purpose for living. He grants to each of us a divine gift to remind us that we have an important part to play.

The Hand of God

I have been a student of the hand of God for many years. Where optimum fruit and vibrant growth once characterized a congregation, I have seen barrenness and mere maintenance take over. I have watched His hand rest on one ministry, and I have watched Him remove His hand from another.

I also have searched for the common denominators in those churches that for decades enjoyed the hand of God on their ministries. One quality in particular showed up repeatedly: the ownership that the people of the church took in the ministry. They didn't wait for a professional or for someone "more qualified" than they. Everyone knew they had a part to play, and they participated gladly. They didn't want God's hand to leave them.

I'm convinced that the influence a church has on its community will be determined in large part not by the personality of the pastor, the size of its building or how long the ministry has worked in the community. It will be determined instead by the percentage of involvement in the ministry of each member. This marks the transition from *attendance* to *ownership*, from being consumers to contributors.

God already has told us that He is not willing that any should perish; therefore, He will not feel satisfied until everyone in our community knows Jesus Christ as Lord and Savior. And if we opt out of His plan, He will find others more willing to jump in.

In the book of Esther, we read how a newly appointed Jewish queen faced the possible annihilation of her people. Mordecai, a close relative, alerts her to a genocidal plot hatched by the wicked Haman. Esther hesitates to get involved; she prefers to take a neutral role. But Mordecai tells her, "If you remain silent at this time, relief and deliverance will arise for the Jews from another place and you and your father's house will perish. And who knows whether you have not attained royalty for such a time as this?" (Esther 4:14).

Mordecai's words stir Esther to action, thus sparing the nation. And due to her involvement—because she used her gift and position well—the Jewish people to this day celebrate the festival of *Purim*, in her honor.

But listen to the phrase that has always challenged me: "If you remain silent at this time, relief and deliverance will arise for the Jews *from another place.*"

Because of His plan for the Messiah's arrival, God remained intent on preserving the Jewish people. He gave Esther the first opportunity to play a vital role in His plan. Deliverance *would* take place. The only question that remained was, What role would she would choose to play in His plan? Would it be a neutral role? Would it be a small part? Would it be a major one? God left the choice up to her, but His plan would come to pass with or without her involvement.

In a similar way, God has a plan for the community where you live and minister today. The only question is, What role will *you* play? People *will* be redeemed. Lives will be transformed. Hopeless marriages will be restored. Lives without direction will be corrected. Yet the question remains: What part will *you* play in His plan?

If we choose to play a major role, God will welcome our involvement. On the other hand, if we choose to remain silent, "help and deliverance will arise from another place." The amount of influence we will have on our generation is up to us. And if we choose poorly, He will open the privilege of involvement to others who are more willing.

We have only one life to live for Christ on this spining earth. This is not *practice*. It's the real thing, and we must seize every opportunity He gives to us. Let us not forget!

Every Member a Minister

God has designed His ministry to be fulfilled, but He leaves the individual roles to our choosing. In doing church as a team, this single principle is the most important one. Ephesians 4:12 (*NKJV*) insists that the saints are to do the "work of ministry."

> *The amount of influence we will have on our generation is up to us. And if we choose poorly, He will open the privilege of involvement to others who are more willing.*

As a boy, I was taught that *saints* were those brave and wonderful Christians of years past who lived miraculously, died for their faith, were canonized and immortalized. But God has a different idea. God calls *every one of us* whom He has chosen to be part of His plan, His "saints." Peter even calls us a "royal priesthood" (1 Pet. 2:9).

Somewhere along the line, we forgot who God created us to be. So instead of fulfilling our own calling, we hire others to do it for us. We interview potential substitutes, and if they can preach and do the business of the church, we give them a job. Then after a few years, if they've done an adequate job of preaching, visiting the sick and performing weddings and funerals, we vote to "renew their call"—so we can step out of their way for another few years.

Doing church as a team is merely a return to the way God designed the church to function. The ministry of the church is not the responsibility of a few professionals; it is the divine responsibility of every one of us.

Every member is a minister; that's what God says. In fact, He calls us to be *full-time* ministers. Full-time? Yes! Not just on Sundays. Not just at Bible studies, but full-time.

How many of us love God just part-time? How many of us want to be in heaven just part-time? We are all full-time citizens of heaven with a commission and an assignment to accomplish during our short stay on this planet.

Before you are a businessman, you are first a full-time minister of Christ. Before you are a homemaker, you are a minister. Before you are a student, a grandparent or a CEO, you are first a minister—a servant of God's purposes during your brief stay on Earth.

Some may protest, "But I don't work for the church! I work for the state (or the police department, a construction company, the department of education, a manufacturing firm). My company pays me, not my church. How can you say that I am a full-time minister?"

Sometimes we mistake the *channel* of our provision for the *source* of our provision. The Bible tells us that God is our provider, not a company or business. If you trace your paycheck back to its true source, it may take you first to your place of employment, but the trail doesn't stop there. If you keep following it, you'll find that all our paychecks can be traced back to the very throne of God. It's like tracing stereo wires to the true source of the music; you might hear notes from the speakers, but they won't provide anything without a solid connection to the amplifier.

God is our provider. He chooses to use various places of employment through which He provides, but it is *He* who provides! Even if you're self-employed, the Bible reminds you, "But you shall remember [there's that word again!] the LORD your God, for it is He who is giving you power to make wealth" (Deut. 8:18).

Why is it, then, that God relays our paychecks to us through our jobs, companies, and places of employment? The answer might surprise you.

What's the Best Way to Reach People?

Doing church as a team comes with a whole new way of looking at this dilemma of reaching people. Do you believe that God loves policemen? I do. Do you believe that He loves teachers? Me, too. What about construction workers? Absolutely! In fact, as we've already seen, the Bible says, "The Lord is . . . not wishing for any to perish but for *all* to come to repentance" (2 Pet. 3:9, emphasis added). So if He truly does love all people and wants to reach them with the gospel, then what would be the very best way to do that?

Through a pastor? Possibly, but that may not be the most ideal. People at your office or school may feel quite intimidated and even put off if a pastor were to walk into the lunch room and begin preaching.

What's the best way to reach teachers? It seems to me that the best way would be through another teacher. So what does God do? He takes full-time ministers and *disguises them* as teachers! He takes saints like you and me and He gives us gifts and a passion to be the best teachers we can be. Then He sends us into the school system where we can reach other educators with God's love.

What about reaching police officers? He takes full-time ministers and *disguises them* as police officers. He gives them all the necessary gifts, passions and credentials, and He assigns them to police departments all over the nation.

How does He reach construction workers? He takes full-time ministers and *disguises them* as construction workers. He gives them the gifts and passions, makes them strong and hairy (excluding female workers, of course!), and He puts them to work at construction sites throughout every city.

God's full-time ministers are *everywhere*. We are *all* ambassadors. We are *all* ministers. Each one of us—not just pastors and evangelists—is called to represent Him in the world. Remember this amazing truth?

> And he determined the times set for them and the exact places where they should live. God did this so that men would seek him and perhaps reach out for him and find him (Acts 17:26,27 *NIV*).

God put you where you are, and He put your church where it is, so that men and women and girls and boys in your neighborhood and within your sphere of influence will have a handy guide around when they seek God and perhaps reach out for Him—in order that they can actually find Him.

I have the privilege of pastoring a young, vibrant church in Hawaii, but my call to this church is no greater a call than the call of anyone else. The pastor's role and responsibilities may differ from other roles, but the callings are the same: *to be ministers for Christ.*

That's why in every city, town and country you will find full-time ministers in every business and vocation. Like salt from a saltshaker, God scatters us everywhere to suit His tastes. He salts the earth with His ministers, giving them various gifts with the power to influence their friends, families and coworkers and, as the old hymn goes, to reach "every kindred, every tribe on this terrestrial ball."[1]

But what good is salt if it doesn't go where it ought to go? What help is it if it doesn't do what it's designed to do? Salt in your gas tank won't do you any favors, nor will a cup of salt in a gallon of seawater do much to sweeten the pot. Salt works to our advantage only when it goes where it should and does what it's designed to do. And if it doesn't, well, Jesus has a word about that:

> You are the salt of the earth; but if the salt has become tasteless, how will it be made salty again? It is good for nothing anymore, except to be thrown out and trampled under foot (Matt. 5:13).

How do you lose your flavor? By forgetting who God made you to be. A memory lapse there means that tastelessness soon follows. So don't lose your flavor, and don't forget who you are!

And who are you? You're a citizen of heaven.

Why are you here? To minister to your neighbors, your coworkers and many others whom God puts in your path, in such a way that they want to know how to become salt themselves.

Don't forget. Remember! And then do something about it.

Team Preparation

1. What important things do you tend to forget?
2. What's the difference between a promise and a covenant? Why is it important to recognize this difference?
3. When did you make the transition from church attendance to ownership, from being a consumer to being a contributor? How do you help others to make this transition?
4. What is your calling as a Christian? How are you fulfilling it?

Note

1. "All Hail the Power of Jesus' Name" (1780), lyrics by Edward Perronet. The verse begins, "Let every kindred, every tribe, on this terrestrial ball, to Him all majesty ascribe, and crown Him Lord of all."

C h a p t e r   4

ALL GOD'S CHILLUN' GOT GIFTS

*Now concerning spiritual gifts, brethren, I do not
want you to be unaware.*

1 CORINTHIANS 12:1

God loves to take ordinary people and through them do extraordinary exploits. He doesn't need superheroes. He is looking for everyday believers, willing vessels that He can equip and gift.

Moreover, God not only gives us these divine endowments but He also supplies the willingness that fuels them. Paul reminds us, "For it is God who is at work in you, both to *will* and to work for His good pleasure" (Phil. 2:13, emphasis added). When we function in the way God has gifted us, not only can we can accomplish great things, but we will also find great joy in doing His will.

Each of us has a God-given capacity to fulfill what He has asked us to accomplish. But our job becomes easier when we locate our niche, our place and our role in the life of the church. Coming to grips with this may be one of the most wonderful discoveries of your life.

Doing church as a team isn't one person doing a hundred things. It's a hundred people doing one thing each—each doing what they do best. Not only is this possible, but it is how God created us.

Cruise Liners and Battleships

Some time ago, our church "adopted" the USS *Reuben James*, a frigate deployed to the Persian Gulf. We agreed to pray daily for the crew and provide the sailors with tapes and books. We also sent them copies of our weekend services so that they could televise them over their internal system on Sunday mornings while at sea.

At the completion of her Gulf tour, the *Reuben James* docked in Pearl Harbor. I received an invitation to become the crew's guest on a short excursion into the Pacific. After a thorough tour of the quarters and decks, I took my place by the captain as we pulled anchor and sailed into the deep blue with a crew of 800. At a safe distance from land, the gunnery detail fired a few rounds from the ship's massive cannons. As every sailor scurried back and forth, I noticed something. Everyone knew exactly what his or her role was. Each person on that ship had a job, a function, a responsibility and a purpose for being there—everyone except me, that is. I was the only one tagging along for the ride.

By contrast, some months later, my wife, Anna, and I took a three-day cruise around the islands for some R&R. On deck, I noticed 400 lazy, sun-ripened human beings lounging around the pool with 40 uniform-clad workers scurrying around trying to keep them happy.

In a moment of reflection I heard the Lord say to me, "My church must be a battleship, not a cruise liner. If you are to pierce the darkness and rescue souls lost on the scratch, you cannot be a ship of spectators. Everyone must know why they are on board."

When you do church as a team, the pastor does *not* do all the work while trying his best to get as many as possible to help him. It's *everyone* doing the work of the ministry, while the pastor is there to equip them.

> *As each one has received a special gift*, employ it in serving one another, as good stewards of the manifold grace of God (1 Pet. 4:10, emphasis added).

Let's take a closer look at how God equips His people. The Bible mentions three basic categories of gifts: office gifts, serving gifts and charismatic gifts.

The Office Gifts

> Therefore it says, "When He ascended on high, He led captive a host of captives, and *He gave gifts to men*." And He gave some as apostles, and some as prophets, and some as evangelists, and some as pastors and teachers, for the *equipping* of the saints for the work of service, to the building up of the body of Christ (Eph. 4:8,11-12, emphasis added).

God established specific offices in the church for the sake of oversight and leadership. Leadership is not reserved exclusively for these positions, but it often gets carried out through them. In doing church as a team, we need to pay special attention to the word "equipping." These offices are not meant to corner the market on ministry, but rather to equip *God's people* to minister.

The Greek word translated "equipping" (*katartismos*) conjures up quite a picture. The term comes from a verb that means, "to mend." We find the word in Mark 1:19, which shows James and John in a boat with their father, Zebedee, *mending* nets. The torn nets may have gotten snagged on the rocky bottom of the Sea of Galilee, so these fishermen mended them prior to their next fishing trip. They were equipping the nets to fulfill the purpose for which they had been created: to catch fish!

In a similar way, hearing the Word of God will often "mend" you. Its truths will impact you in such a way that God brings wholeness and healing to a hurting area of your life or to your relationships. Through reading God's Word, you become increasingly equipped for the purposes to which God has called you. Its messages challenge you, reminding you of who you are, and call you to boldly use the gifts He has given you.

A fisherman does not mend his nets in order to increase his collection of marine memorabilia. Neither is his goal to compete with other fishermen to see who can accumulate the biggest pile of equipment. That would be ludicrous! Fishermen don't mend nets to display them on a wall as trophies. So why does a fisherman mend his torn nets?

To throw them back in the sea to catch more fish!

A few years ago, we wanted to expand our counseling ministry, so our counseling department held training sessions for new recruits. How exciting to see more than 80 men and women attend the training classes! After participating in a 12-

week class, every student graduated.

A year later, we offered the class again. This time, 50 signed up. The leaders got so excited that they concluded God was telling them to offer the course every year.

Not long afterward, some members of our staff approached me with a request for more paid counselors. The weekly load had greatly increased and our staff simply could not keep up with the demand. So I asked them, "What about the 80 who took the counselor's training? And the 50? Where are they?"

I found out that *none* of them were doing any counseling. Instead, the staff was considering a Counselor's Training II for those who had graduated from Counselor's Training I. They were laboring under the misconception that since they had taught a class, they had fulfilled their counseling assignment. What was designed to be a *means* had become an end in itself.

Equipping others is not an end in itself. It is a means! Not until the saints are serving and doing the actual work of the ministry have pastors completed their assignment.

God equips us to "go into all the world and preach the gospel to all creation" (Mark 16:15). He strengthens us that we may discover and develop our gifts, and then employ them "in serving one another" (1 Pet. 4:10). Paul says that as we do, the Body of Christ gets built up (see Eph. 4:12).

That's how churches grow! When our people are being consistently mended and equipped by the Word of God so that *they do the work of the ministry*, churches become vibrant and healthy.

The Serving Gifts

And since we have gifts that differ according to the grace given to us, let each exercise them accordingly: if prophecy, according to the proportion of his faith; if service, in his serving; or he who teaches, in his teaching; or he who exhorts, in his exhortation; he who gives, with liberality; he who leads, with diligence; he who shows mercy, with cheerfulness (Rom. 12:6-8).

God distributes service gifts among Christians to equip us to excel in serving. Merely knowing what they are, however, will not help us much. We must go beyond discovery to developing and deploying these gifts if they are to be of any use to anyone.

If God says that your gift is teaching, then you must teach. If your gift is serving, then by all means, find a place and start serving. If your gift is leading, then for the sake of the kingdom of God, lead. To possess a gift and not use it is unthinkable and unacceptable to God.

Each of us must take responsibility to exercise our gifts. *As each of us discovers and begins to use our gifts, God is honored, the Body of Christ is built up, and we begin to know a sense of fulfillment greater than any we can find in the world.*

I know too many believers who have wonderful talents, great training, fine education and a stellar heritage, who nevertheless sit in the pews every week, eager to get in and out of church without being recognized. They don't use their gifts and they refuse to get involved—and over the years they become sour, sarcastic and cynical.

The apostle Paul had a very different lifelong goal: to discover the reason for his God-ordained birth.

Not that I have already obtained it, or have already become perfect, but I press on in order that I may lay hold of that for which also I was laid hold of by Christ Jesus (Phil. 3:12).

Paul expressed his gift of apostleship in his passion to pioneer churches and to take the gospel to the Gentiles. God had chosen him for a specific purpose, gifted him for a specific reason, and Paul had no intention of going home (to heaven) until he had fulfilled the task for which God had laid hold of him.

The Charismatic Gifts

Now there are varieties of gifts, but the same Spirit. For to one is given the word of wisdom through the Spirit, and to another the word of knowledge . . . to another faith by the same Spirit, and to another gifts of healing . . . to another the effecting of miracles, and to another prophecy, and to another the distinguishing of spirits, to another various kinds of tongues, and to another the interpretation of tongues. But one and the same Spirit works all these things, distributing to each one individually just as He wills (1 Cor. 12:4,8-11).

The charismatic gifts have long been the focus of tremendous controversy. Various interpretations of this passage of Scripture have divided churches, segregated congregations and generally caused more havoc than whether a Christian should "smoke, chew or hang around with girls who do."

God has authored every gift by His Spirit and placed them in the church for the common good. Each congregation is designed to have a balance, with all the gifts represented and all the gifts functioning. Every gift—big or small, seen or unseen, on the platform or in the background—is crucial to a church's ability to operate with optimum effectiveness. To misunderstand this aspect of the church is like trying to run a computer program with some of the program data missing. It just won't function as it should, and it will cause more frustration than gratitude.

But what did we do? Somewhere along the way, we embraced all the gifts that *looked like us* and quarantined all the rest. All those with certain gifts, such as tongues, miracles and prophecy, were grouped together under the label "charismatic" or "Pentecostal." These folks so enjoyed each other's company that they began creating denominations based on the similarity of their gifts.

> *God never said, "Find a church where everyone in it looks like you." We are to find a church where everyone looks like* Him!

Others gathered themselves according to the serving gifts (see Rom. 12:6-8) and became known as the "conservative" wing of the church. They emphasized such gifts as teaching and leadership, serving and giving.

For years, these two factions drew their lines, took their firing pins off safety, and never the twain would meet. Certain gifts became badges of honor, measurements of spirituality and terms of endearment.

Often, Christians use similarity and familiarity as measuring rods for evaluating a church. If we enter a new church and they sing, talk, preach and act like us, that church passes the test and we consent to have fellowship with them. On the other hand, if the congregation doesn't meet our expectations, then we conclude that this congregation comes up lacking in the spiritually sound department, and so we deem them unworthy of our involvement.

But God never said, "Find a church where everyone in it looks like you." We are to find a church where everyone looks like *Him*!

Thank God, the kind of segregated thinking that has separated churches from one another is beginning to disappear. The Lord's original design called for all the gifts to function together, in harmony and with mutual respect. Every gift is necessary to accomplish what He desires with His people. No one of us alone will possess all the gifts, but altogether, we do.

There's nothing like the church when it works as God designed it to, resulting in a vibrant, healthy and joyful family.

Welcome to the Church!

At New Hope Christian Fellowship, we welcome the totality of the gifts of the Holy Spirit as God designed them to function. We have many with the gift of serving, some with the gift of tongues, others with the gifts of leadership, teaching, mercy, giving, and the rest.

We must strive to use our gifts in biblical, loving ways, respecting each other as men and women made in God's image. Of course, selfish motives can tarnish what God designed, but to discard the usage of certain gifts for fear of this happening would be the greatest misuse of all.

When a person needs prayer, we all pray, but there's nothing like someone with a *gift* of intercession who will pray with passion until the request is answered (and it usually is).

When we need someone to oversee the hospital ministry,

those with a mercy gift will usually step forward first (and the patients rejoice).

When groups in the church reach an impasse and can't seem to make a necessary decision, we call upon those with the gift of leadership, and they respond with great joy. The impasse gets broken and the church moves forward again.

When we need to get things organized, those with the gift of organization get excited. They gladly step up and create phenomenal things from what had appeared to be nothing but chaos.

When we need facilities set up or when we need to get a room prepared for an activity, those with the gift of serving make themselves willing and ready.

Some time ago, I was to gather a few pastors for a morning meeting. I asked my administrative assistant, Carol Ann, if she would put some pitchers of water on the tables and enough cups to serve those I had invited. Carol Ann is an outstanding recruiter of people according to their gifts, so instead of doing something just to get by, she called Neta.

Now, Neta's gift is hospitality, so when Carol Ann asked her to help, she felt overjoyed and went right to work. She picked fresh flowers and lined the tables with beautiful tablecloths. She filled water pitchers with ice-cold water and she placed a color-coordinated scarf on each, as if this were a competition for contemporary décor. She placed specially selected nuts on each table, with candies and napkins adorning the individual place settings. The whole room took on a new appearance and the aroma of fresh coffee, bagels and pastries filled the air. Neta spent a full day preparing the room and making sure the ambiance was just right—and she loved doing it!

When I walked into the room the morning of the meeting, I thought I had stumbled into a photo shoot for *Better Homes and*

Gardens. It absolutely stunned me. The visiting pastors felt so special that *I* would take the time to organize such a beautiful setting for our meeting. Frankly, if it had been left to me, they would have found a stack of paper cups on each table and a note that they could retrieve their own water from the fountain downstairs.

But all the credit went to Neta. After the meeting, Neta came up and asked, "Do you think you might be having any more of these meetings soon? I just love doing these things!"

As I said, Neta's gift is hospitality.

If it weren't for each of us being willing and ready to use our individual gifts for the common good, our church would soon be in deep trouble. The more that people serve one another through the willing use of their gifts, the more the respect factor for one another grows until it shoots through the roof.

We really do need each other.

The Danger of Comparison

One common pitfall hinders many from finding their place in the Body of Christ: comparison. We start focusing on the gifts we don't possess rather than using the ones we do have. We try to look like, sound like and think like the people we admire most. In the end, this leads only to frustration and a half-baked, mediocre version of the gifting we tried so hard to imitate.

And you know the worst part of this? Our own creative energies start to dry up. It's always easier to duplicate than it is to incarnate. But God wants to use the specific ways He created us to bring a sparkle to the things God has asked us to be a part of.

My wife, Anna, is from Springfield, Oregon. Some years ago, the Springfield Public Schools newsletter published a story that Chuck Swindoll mentioned in his wonderful book *Growing*

Strong in the Seasons of Life. The story reminds us of how the Master Architect has uniquely designed each one of us.

Once upon a time, the animals decided they should do something meaningful to meet the problems of the new world. So they organized a school. They adopted an activity curriculum of running, climbing, swimming and flying. To make it easier to administer, all the animals took all the subjects.

The duck was excellent in swimming. In fact, he was better than his instructor! However, he made only passing grades in flying, and was very poor in running. Since he was so slow in running, he had to drop swimming and stay after school to practice running. This caused his webbed feet to be badly worn so he became only average in swimming. But "average" was quite acceptable, therefore nobody worried about it—except the duck.

The rabbit started at the top of his class in running, but he developed a nervous twitch in his leg muscles because he had so much makeup work to do in swimming.

The squirrel was excellent in climbing, but he encountered constant frustration in flying class because his teacher made him start from the ground up instead of from the treetop down. He developed "charley horses" from overexertion, so he only got a "C" in climbing and a "D" in running.

The eagle was a problem child and was severely disciplined for being a nonconformist. In climbing classes, he beat all the others to the top but insisted on using his own way of getting there![1]

The moral of this story? Each of us has been given unique gifts, capabilities and passions, which enable us to excel in certain activities. If we concentrate on pointing out each other's weaknesses, however, we may seem spiritual or vigilant. but we won't be fruitful or very helpful.

As I like to say, *everybody is a 10—somewhere.*

When we compare ourselves with one another, we can also become blinded to the wonderful qualities God has woven into our own design. A better way would be for each of God's creatures to develop his or her own gifts, while at the same time learning to respect the gifts of others.

God isn't into making clones. We are not all the same; He never intended for us to be. God placed each of us in His family with a certain mixture of gifts, temperaments and capabilities. When we operate within our individual roles and realms of gifting, we will find it much easier (and more likely) to excel. Not only will we tremendously benefit the Body of Christ, but we will also experience incredible joy.

In order to accomplish what God has intended for us as individuals and as a whole, we must do church as a team. A 99 percent involvement is still 1 percent shy. We need all of us functioning in our gifts, with respect and love for each other. That's what the local church body is all about! No one is unimportant. Everyone, not just the pastor, is a part of sharing the gospel. We do church as a team!

Booker T. Washington, the most influential black leader and educator of his time in America, once said, "No race can prosper till it learns that there is as much dignity in tilling a field as in writing a poem."[2] If I understand correctly what he said, it is this: *Every person is incredibly important to the fulfillment of God's plan.* Take hold of that! *No one is unimportant.* Let that truth burn within your soul. The ministry belongs to you and me, and it requires both of us. Doing church is not the responsibility of the professional clergy and a few talented staff people; it is the privilege of all of us—together.

You don't find the strength of a church in the beauty of its building, the number of attendees or the size of its budget. A church is only as strong as the involvement of its members; and the more each person takes ownership in the ministry of the church, the stronger it becomes. Only when we realize that God has called every one of us with an equally divine imperative can the church at large and our individual congregations begin to reach their fullest potential.

So relax! Enjoy who God created you to be. Rest in Him. Cultivate your gifts and God-given capabilities. Don't compare yourself with others, and don't worry about what you don't have. Instead, put to use what you *do* have. Don't bemoan your weaknesses, but strengthen your strengths!

There's plenty of room for every creature, every gift and every style. Don't settle for a stack of paper cups and a note directing you to the water cooler when you can enjoy scarf-draped pitchers of ice water and a gorgeous scene straight out of *Better Homes and Gardens*. You'll be far better off—and so will the people who get to use their gifts in the service of the living God.

Team Preparation

1. Each Christian has at least one spiritual gift. Look up the following Scripture verses. What does each one tell us about the gifts?
    a. 1 Corinthians 12:1
    b. Romans 12:6-8
    c. 1 Corinthians 12:4,8-11

    d. Ephesians 4:8-12

2. Why do you think the issue of spiritual gifts has divided the church?

3. What is your understanding of how the gifts should operate together in any one church? Should the gifts be segregated? Why or why not?

4. What are your spiritual gifts? How do you know? List them below.

5. With your gifts in mind, in what possible ministries would you fit well?

6. If you could do any ministry at all in the local church that would make every day seem like Christmas for you, which ministry would you choose?

Notes

1. Chuck Swindoll, *Growing Strong in the Seasons of Life* (Sisters, OR: Multnomah Publishers, 1984), p. 312.

2. Booker T. Washington, *Up from Slavery* (1901), quoted in John Bartlett, *Familiar Quotations*, 15th edition, p. 681.

C h a p t e r   5

FINDING
YOUR FIT

For it is God who works in you to will and to act
according to his good purpose.

PHILIPPIANS 2:13, *NIV*

Each of us is like a piece in a giant jigsaw puzzle; every piece has
its place in God's plan. No piece is optional. How frustrating it
would be to put together a 3,000-piece puzzle, only to find one
piece missing at the end!

That's how God sees us, as a wonderful puzzle made up
entirely of incredibly important pieces. Everyone is necessary to
complete the divine puzzle. When all the pieces fit together, the
world can see a beautiful, completed portrait of the heart of
Jesus, beating for people everywhere.

But how do we find our place in God's plan? Will it come
easily? Where do we start? As with most puzzles, no piece falls

smoothly into place on the first attempt. It usually takes several tries in order to find the right fit. You turn the piece this way and that, set it aside and try a few others, and then you try it again. If a piece doesn't fit on the first go-round, you don't toss the rebellious part in the trash! No, you keep going because you know every piece is a perfect fit—somewhere.

But I am just one piece, you might rationalize. *They can do without me. Why, there are 2,999 other pieces! I'm just one, insignificant piece. They'll never miss me.*

Don't you dare think that way! That's exactly how the enemy of our souls wants you to think, but don't you do it—even for a minute. You are vital to the success of God's plan and mission.

Remember, everyone is a 10—somewhere.

Breaking Through Our Limitations

Each of us knows what it means to have someone (or maybe even ourselves) sentence us to some major life limitation. Artificial limitations might result from a painful upbringing, difficult circumstances, a parent's hurtful comments, terrible failures and even the callous judgment of our friends. These mental ceilings restrain us from discovering our fullest potential.

But God makes His power available to every one of us. He remains able even when we are not. He is strong when we are weak and, regardless of how we feel, God always provides a way. If we are going to become what God has designed us to be, then we must discover these false ceilings in our lives and break through them.

Have you ever been to a circus and seen elephants perform? These mighty beasts possess incredible strength. When I was 10 years old, I spotted one of these awesome creatures outside the

big top, and in my innocent way, I crawled under the rope to get
a closer look. It shocked me to see this huge elephant restrained
only by a tiny rope attached to a foot-long stake barely pounded
into the dirt. The monstrous pachyderm would wander the full
length of the rope and, when it felt a little tug, it would stop.
With one flick of its huge foot, the elephant could have sent that
stake flying through the air (and flattened me) with the greatest
of ease. But it never tried.

Later, I asked a caretaker about this. He explained that when
an elephant is very young, its owners tie it to a very strong stake,
hammered deep into the ground. After pulling and tugging on
the restraint to no avail, the elephant eventually figures that further attempts to get loose will result only in futility and aggra-
vation. So the elephant give up trying. When that elephant
grows into an adult, it still has this limitation in its mind.
(Remember, an elephant never forgets!) Now all the caretaker
has to do is to put a little stake in the ground, attach a flimsy
rope to the animal's foot, and the elephant won't go anywhere.
Why? Because it doesn't believe that it can! The huge animal has
been conditioned to think small.

How much potential do you have? How willing are you to
reach for God's fullest measure? Let's take a look at your potential for a moment.

All You Can Do, But Haven't Done Yet

Your potential is like an iceberg, with 10 percent of its mass
floating above the water while the other 90 percent hides
beneath the surface. You have the potential of that whole iceberg—but most of us use only the 10 percent above the waterline.
With God's help, you can put your whole potential to its fullest
use for the Lord.

Potential is like power on idle; it is latent energy. Potential is all you can become, but haven't become quite yet. It is all you can do, but haven't done yet. It is everywhere you can go, haven't gone there yet. Paul the apostle said in Philippians 3:12-14, "I press on so that I may lay hold of that for which also I was laid hold of by Christ Jesus. Brethren, I do not regard myself as having laid hold of it yet; but one thing I do: forgetting what lies behind and reaching forward to what lies ahead, I press on toward the goal for the prize of the upward call of God in Christ Jesus."

I wonder—what's inside of you? What latent gifts reside within you right now?

Use the following blanks to rate yourself on how much of your potential you have reached. Write a percentage in the space next to each category. How do you fare? Where are you right now in each of the following categories?

1. Spiritual growth   _____

2. Personal growth   _____

3. Financial health   _____

4. People skills   _____

5. Physical health   _____

6. Vocational abilities   _____

7. Family health   _____

8. As a leader in church   _____

9. Relationship with friends   _____

Finding Your Design

God doesn't want you to settle for anything less than His very best. You have been created with special talents, abilities and gifts. That's wonderful, but even more important is how you invest them. Only when you put them into action will you be able to crash through your barriers of limitation.

Many wonderful courses can help you find your gifts and passions. At New Hope, we often use the DESIGN course to help us determine our gift mix. We teach this course regularly both at our church and at our annual Doing Church as a Team conferences. You can also find one of these tests online at www.enewhope.org.

We offer no guarantees that a person will pinpoint his or her full mixture of gifts by graduation, but I do guarantee that each participant will come away with a much greater appreciation and understanding of his or her gifts. The more you understand the way the Lord designed you, the better you will be able to cooperate with that design.

DESIGN is an acrostic that represents the different ingredients that, once combined, equal *you*. When you recognize and develop each of these six categories, you'll be on your way to realizing and developing your full potential in Christ.

D for Desire

What is your passion? If all things were equal and you could do anything in the world for the Lord, what job would you choose—something that would make every day feel like Christmas for you? God has placed certain desires in you as one way of telling you what He wants you to do. He has given you not only certain abilities, but also the desire to pursue exactly what He's asked you to do. Philippians 2:13 tells us, "It is God who is at work in you, both to *will* and to *work for* His good pleasure" (emphasis added). And 1 Timothy 3:1 says, "Here is a trustworthy saying: If anyone *sets his heart* on being an overseer, he *desires* a noble task"

(*NIV*, emphasis added). The kind of heart desire that Paul describes in this verse spills over into far more than the longing to become a church leader; it pictures the kind of longing that God pairs with all of His gifts. The gifts God gives come with a passion to use them; passion is the divine exclamation point that comes with using what God bestows on us. So along with special gifts, God also gives to each of us certain passions—arenas of service that motivate us more than others.

We've all seen musicians who have a passion for the piano, above all other musical instruments. Therefore, they play piano with a passion.

We've all seen gifted athletes who perform in outstanding ways in one particular sport. They may possess the ability to excel in many different venues, but one sport catches their fancy more than the others do, and that is where they pour all their time and energy. They excel in that sport and play it with passion.

Your passion is the area, or arena, where you feel most motivated to use your gift. *Knowing your spiritual gift will answer the* **what** *question; knowing your passion will answer the* **where** *questions*:

- Where shall I use my gifts?
- Where do I feel most motivated to serve?
- Where do I sense a calling or an attraction?

While some may have the gift of serving, their *passion* is to help elderly people—so they minister to the needs of senior citizens. Others may have the gift of teaching, while their *passion* is discipleship—so they feel drawn to small-group ministry. Others may find they have a gift in music, while their passion is working with children—so they lead music in the children's ministry.

Once you link your gifts with your passion, you will begin to play a powerful role in the Body of Christ and will find great joy and motivation in your service. When you operate in your gift and passion, you will enjoy maximum effectiveness with a minimum of weariness.

> *When you operate in your gift and passion, you will enjoy maximum effectiveness with a minimum of weariness.*

On the other hand, when you do *not* operate in your gift and passion, you will experience maximum weariness with a minimum of effectiveness. I'm sure every person reading this book has felt that kind of strain at one time or another!

E for Experience

Your experiences are important considerations when seeking and finding your design. What tasks or projects have influenced you? God will use even negative experiences to complete your design. What have you learned from the times when you have been hurt? How have they made you more compassionate toward others in similar situations?

God will never waste a hurt. One of my favorite Bible verses is Psalm 56:8: "Thou hast taken account of my wanderings; put my tears in Thy bottle; are they not in Thy book?" (*KJV*).

God has put all your tears in a bottle. He remembers them all and will use them for your good. Some people think that because of their past or the way they were raised, they will find it impossible to succeed in this world. Yet consider a few examples of people who overcame such obstacles. You may recognize some of these names.

He didn't talk till he was four years old and didn't start to read till he was seven. One of his teachers labeled him "mentally slow, unsociable and adrift in his foolish dreams." This was often said of young *Albert Einstein*.

"He's too stupid to learn anything," said some teachers of a young boy named *Thomas Edison*.

"He possesses minimal football knowledge and lacks motivation," an expert said of a beginning coach named *Vince Lombardi*.

He went bankrupt several times and was fired by the editor of a local newspaper because of an apparent lack of ideas. The man they fired was *Walt Disney*.

He failed the sixth grade and suffered a lifetime of setbacks and defeats. Finally, as a senior citizen, *Winston Churchill* became the prime minister of England.

Don't let setbacks keep you from excelling in the very areas where God has gifted you to achieve astonishing success. Who knows what amazing things He has planned for you to achieve, if only you will develop and use the gifts He's lavished on you?

S for Spiritual Gift

Every person who knows Jesus Christ is endowed with one or more spiritual gifts. These are described in 1 Corinthians 12, Romans 12, Ephesians 4 and 1 Peter 4. God never intended for Christ's ministry to cease when He ascended into heaven, so He decided that His ministry would be carried on through those who believed. Knowing that we could never do it on our own, God sent His Spirit, who distributed gifts to the church, through which we carry on His work.

What are your spiritual gifts? Are you willing for God to use you in any of them? For example, Romans 12 lists the following gifts; you have at least one of these. Take a look.

1. *Prophecy:* The ability to discern quickly between right and wrong. This gift compels this believer to see things without shades of gray.
2. *Serving:* This person feels motivated to meet physical needs through serving. Whether it is helping set up chairs, sweeping floors, cooking, or any of the manifold needs that arise, this person feels comfortable and motivated to help in this way.
3. *Teaching:* A person with a teaching gift enjoys sharing truths with others and loves to discover what helps others to most effectively learn.
4. *Exhortation:* An exhorter enjoys the process of communicating in order to stir another's faith to higher levels. He or she sees the steps necessary to resolve a problem or move a ministry forward. He or she is able to garner support and mobilize people toward a common goal.
5. *Giving:* A person with the gift of giving feels motivated to meet a need or advance a ministry by removing any financial burden that would impede its progress. He or she takes great delight in financially supporting a worthy ministry.
6. *Leading:* A leader has the ability to administrate and organize others toward a common goal or direction.

7. *Mercy:* Those with the gift of mercy are able to quickly discern the emotional hurts of others. They feel motivated to alleviate the inner struggles in others, even more than meet their physical needs.

Each of us has at least one of these motivational gifts that will fuel our actions and tendencies. *But as important as each one is, they become unbalanced if operated in isolation. Each one requires the addition and contributions of the other six gifts, working in sync with one another.*

If you would like some help in discovering your own gift mix, I invite you to take our online test at www.enewhope.org. It should help you to get moving in a positive direction in this crucial area.

I for Individual Style

Each of us has a unique temperament reflected in what we usually call our personality or individual style. On one end of the scale are the extroverts, while at the other end of the spectrum live the introverts. You might be a strong extrovert or a mild introvert; we wind up all over the scale.

We all know "people persons," and others who seem more task-oriented. Some live very structured lives, while others are impetuous and spontaneous.

Extroverts and introverts who have given their lives to Christ have one thing in common: they both love people. Yet there is a big difference in how they react after loving others. After being with people for an extended time, an introvert feels drained and needs to have his or her emotional batteries recharged; to do that, he or she needs to pull away from people for a time. Extroverts, on the other hand, feel their batteries charging up in the presence of others; their emotional batteries quickly drain in periods of isolation. To get recharged, they have to get back with people.

In order to pace yourself with others, you must discover how you're wired. Every person will need to discern his own temperamental balance, as it affects how you are best able to do ministry.

I am a mild introvert, so I can be with people for a long stretch, but I need to take a break about every six weeks and crawl into a cave for three or four days. My "Sabbaths" require not only one day in seven, but three days after six weeks.

I have never been a salesman. I remember a time when I was supposed to sell tickets for a school project. I begged my dad to buy them all, so I wouldn't have to sell them door-to-door. Another time I took all the money I had saved in order to pay for a case of almond chocolates our school was selling—25 bars at a dollar per bar! Later, I gave them away as gifts.

When I became a Christian in college, I attended a course in evangelism held by Campus Crusade for Christ, an outstanding group founded by Bill Bright. Crusade perfected and published *The Four Spiritual Laws*, a little booklet used to win millions to Christ. I spent one entire morning learning how to use this booklet. Then came the moment of truth. For our final project, we were to go door-to-door and for the last two hours share the Four Spiritual Laws with our neighbors. I wanted to die! All the other students seemed so excited, and I felt like such a worm because I didn't want to win anyone to the Lord.

While everyone else zealously banged on doors, I quietly found a McDonald's nearby, read my Bible for two hours and repented that I couldn't bring myself to lead anyone to the Lord. When everyone returned with glowing reports, I just sat there in the corner of the room, hoping no one would notice me. I felt guilty and condemned.

On the other hand, I love the arts. I love music, creative multimedia presentations, storytelling and songwriting. Over the years, I've pursued these with a passion. In Bible college, I formed a musical group that traveled throughout the country each summer, singing and speaking at dozens of youth camps. Through the use of the arts and through public speaking, I have seen hundreds of people come to Christ. During the first year of New Hope in Oahu, God allowed me to play a small part in seeing more than 1,800 people receive Christ for the first time. I felt humbled to learn this; it is equivalent of five people a day being won to Christ! Even at the time of this writing, more than 3,500 people receive Christ each year through our weekend services.

My calling remains the same, although my design will dictate the style best suited to helping me achieve excellent results. Your individual style will not change your calling as a Christian, but it will suggest how to best carry out your calling. Each of us must run the race set before us. We each do it differently, but the main thing is to actually *run the race!*

G for Growth Phase

God calls us to grow in Christ as long as we walk this earth. Therefore, each of us is still growing in the Lord. Some of us may be spiritual toddlers, while others have reached the adolescent or adult stage. Adolescents may have knowledge but still have a long way to go in gaining wisdom—that is, the ability to apply their knowledge to everyday living. Others are fountains of common, street sense, but know very little of the Bible.

Many people mistakenly believe that spiritual growth can be measured by the number of hours spent in church. But the truth is that in one or two years, a person intent on following the Lord can become much more mature and laden with insight and wisdom than another Christian who has remained on cruise-control throughout a decade of noninvolvement.

Don't forget that Jesus turned over the responsibility for administrating the whole church to a few former fishermen and tax gatherers *just three years old in the Lord!* Christian growth is better measured more by a person's willingness to apply what he has heard than by his length of stay in the pews. John 13:17 reminds us, "If you know these things, you are blessed if you *do* them" (emphasis added).

Are you an infant, toddler, adolescent, young adult or a mature adult in your relationship with Christ? Your current growth phase factors in as part of your DESIGN and gives you valuable insight into where you can best plug into the ministry of your church.

N for Natural Abilities

All of us have seen natural athletes who appear to excel in any sport they take up. Other people have natural abilities in other areas, such as computers, working with children, mechanics, electronics or problem solving. Our natural abilities add an important component of who God made us to be.

What do you enjoy doing? Do you have a natural talent for fixing things? What about strategic planning, financial planning, working with the elderly or working with babies? When we work within our design, life gets exciting and fun.

God isn't some unbending drillmaster who demands your service. He really wants your heart! He tells us in Deuteronomy 28:47-48, "Because you did not serve the LORD your God with joy and a glad heart, for the abundance of all things; therefore you shall serve your enemies." You see, God doesn't want us merely to serve Him; He wants us to serve Him *joyfully*. Then we will function in the way God designed us to function. If you feel miserable and resentful serving cookies to three-year-olds, then just maybe God didn't design you for that task. You'll be a lot better off—and so will your church—if you give up your duties in the toddler department and search for something that you actually enjoy. Find what you like to do and where you can excel, and do it with all your heart!

Add all these components together, and you'll find your DESIGN. These ingredients will help you to find the shape and placement of your puzzle piece. Now all you need to add to this recipe is involvement!

Patience: The Breakfast of Champions

Finding your fit may take time. Be patient. God may want to build your quality of character before He fits you into your niche. In any case, be patient. Everything has an order to it, and we can't push our way into God's plan.

When most people start on a puzzle, they begin by fitting the edge pieces together, forming a frame. The frame is the easiest part of the puzzle to assemble because each of the border pieces has at least one side with a straight edge. Once you get those together, then you start working your way toward the middle.

Finding your fit in a church often resembles this process. Just like fitting the pieces of a puzzle together, it requires patience. Sometimes you'll see others getting assigned to tasks almost immediately. When that happens, you might feel tempted to label these people as part of the "in crowd," while you struggle with feeling like an outsider.

Relax! Just as it takes awhile to get to the inner pieces of a puzzle, so it may take you awhile to find your best fit. Be patient—you may not be able to find your fit until two or three other edge pieces find theirs. Then, lo and behold, you might very well be that piece that joins them all together! But until that happens, work on your character. Develop the *fruit* of the Spirit as you work to discover where you fit with the *gifts* of the Spirit.

Galatians 5:22-23 gives us the famous list: "But the fruit of the Spirit is love, joy, peace, patience, kindness, goodness, faithfulness, gentleness, and self control." Take time to develop each of these character qualities. Without them, you will quickly (and repeatedly) run into personality conflicts and step into relational potholes that will impede your ministry and life. When God has you in His waiting room, it is for a important reason. He is not stalling. He is not slow about His promises (2 Pet. 3:9). He is not marginalizing you. He is working on you and is asking you to cooperate with Him. He must position you for his best, and He will not put you in a place for which you are unprepared.

Be patient. Don't give up. Don't think that you are unimportant or forgotten. And do not surrender to self-defeating thoughts that since you are not "needed" right now, then you must be insignificant: "They have lots of servants here in this church. They don't need me. After all, I am just one person and this church has so many more qualified people than me!"

Don't think that way for one moment! You might be surprised at the power of just one. You can make a huge difference!

- In 1645, one vote gave Oliver Cromwell control of England.
- In 1776, one vote made English the official language of the United States instead of German, at least according to folklore.
- In 1845, one vote brought Texas into the Union. Later, California, Oregon, Washington and Idaho were

admitted to the Union and the purchase of Alaska was ratified—all by a single vote.

- In 1868, one vote saved President Andrew Johnson from being impeached.
- In 1876, one vote gave Rutherford B. Hayes the U.S. presidency.
- In 1923, one vote gave Adolph Hitler control of the Nazi Party.[1]

You are just one, but you count. Remember, everybody is a 10—somewhere. And most definitely that includes you!

Team Preparation

1. Using the DESIGN acrostic, list personal characteristics that would best identify you.

   Desire:

   Experience:

   Spiritual gift:

   Individual style:

   Growth phase:

   Natural abilities:

2. Where do you think you would best fit in the ministries of your church? Where do you really enjoy serving?

Notes

1. Mary W. Morgan, "The Importance of One Vote," *Collier County Government Services*, revised June 29, 2000. http://www.co.collier.fl.us/elec tions/onevote.htm (accessed August 7, 2000). Morgan is the former supervisor of elections for Collier County, Florida.

Chapter 6

THE FASTEST
WAY TO THE
THRONE

But when you are invited, go and recline at the last place, so that
when the one who has invited you comes, he may say to you, "Friend,
move up higher"; then you will have honor in the sight of all who are
at the table with you. For everyone who exalts himself shall be humbled,
and he who humbles himself shall be exalted.

LUKE 14:10-11

At New Hope we love to tell each other, "The fastest way to the throne will always be through the servant's entrance." We mean that regardless of a person's gifts, talents or abilities, each of us is called to the foot of the table.

Jesus modeled servanthood for us, and when we develop our

gifts, we begin by coming through the servant's entrance. That's more a matter of the heart than it is a matter of giftedness. Whatever the need is, we must be willing to pick up a towel and wash someone's feet. It may not feel glamorous, but hey, there's no quicker way to get to the throne.

No Guarantee of Blessing

God calls you to serve Him by using your gifts through the church, but do you want to know something? Merely using your gifts does not guarantee that God will bless you. Does that surprise you? The truth is, if you really want God's blessing, then you must use your gifts with the right heart and the right motives.

Sometimes people use gifting to justify their behavior. If a distasteful job has to be done, a person may say, "Oh, that just isn't my gift. That's not my passion." When that happens, usually it is not an issue of gifts or passions, but an issue of the heart.

Each of us has a tendency to use religious cloaks to justify selfish motives. This is nothing new. All our lives, the arrows of attention and interest have been turned inward, and some of those arrows are difficult to redirect. Turning them away from ourselves takes daily effort and a constant commitment to purity and the development of a servant heart.

The late Mother Teresa has often spoken to my heart through her books. This incredible leader exemplified for me the untiring heart of a servant. In her classic book *The Love of Christ*, Mother Teresa speaks of her magnificent work in Calcutta. She reflects:

What we are doing is but a drop in the ocean. This may

be only a drop, but the ocean would be less if it weren't there. What we do is something small, but we do it with big hearts. At death, we will not be judged by the amount of work we did, but by the amount of love we put into it. We do not strive for spectacular actions. What counts is the gift of yourself, the degree of love you put into each of your deeds. . . . Do you want to be great? Pick up a broom and sweep the floor.[1]

I love that! Here was a servant whom God used to touch a needy world. She felt content to serve an "Audience of One," as Greg Ferguson so aptly described it. She didn't clean tables with a washcloth; she cleaned them with her heart. She didn't give speeches with eloquence; she gave them with her heart.

When you serve, serve with your heart. Whether you teach, sing, pass out bulletins, play an instrument, set up chairs or clean tables, always remember: *It's not the size of the task but the size of the heart you put into the task that makes what you do something beautiful for God.*

And then you're ready for blessing—more than you can imagine!

Three Blessings of Using Your Gifts

God designed each of us to get intimately involved in His plan. When you willingly launch out and use your gifts for the sake of the Kingdom—and with the right heart—three wonderful things begin to happen. You will

- know amazing joy,
- enjoy healthy accountability, and
- experience accelerated spiritual growth.

Amazing Joy

Converting your potential into reality results in amazing joy. The Greek word for spiritual gifts is *charismata*, which is derived from the word *charis*, or grace. And the root word of grace? It is the word *chara*, which means joy. Joy lives at the very root of the proper use of your spiritual gift!

In his book *Anatomy of an Illness*, Norman Cousins tells about the latter years of Pablo Casals, one of the great musicians of the twentieth century. On the morning of his 90th birthday, Casals's arthritis and frailty made it almost unbearable to watch him begin his day. His emphysema afflicted him with heavy, labored breathing. Casals walked with a shuffle, stooped over with his head pitched forward. His hands were swollen, his fingers clenched, and he looked every inch a very tired old man.

But that day, even before eating breakfast, Pablo Casals made his way to the piano, one of the instruments on which he had become proficient. Laboriously and with great difficulty, he arranged himself on the piano bench. It seemed like such a terrible effort for him to bring his clenched, swollen fingers to the keyboard.

Then something miraculous happened. Casals began to undergo a complete transformation. As he played this instrument he so loved, moving where he was so gifted, his very physiology changed and produced in his body (and on the piano) a result that seemed possible only for a strong, healthy individual. His fingers slowly unclenched and reached for the keys, like the tendrils of a plant reaching toward the sunlight. Casals began with a rendition of Bach, then moved on to a Brahms concerto, racing his fingers across the keyboard. His whole body seemed to fuse with the music. His frame looked no longer stiff and shrunken, but graceful and completely free from its arthritic bondage.

By the time he walked away from the piano, Casals seemed an entirely different person. He stood taller and walked without a trace of a shuffle. He immediately moved to the breakfast table, ate a hearty meal and then went out for a stroll along the beach.[2]

What a wonderful story of belief and renewal! It graphically illustrates how God has designed us to use our gifts. We can exchange labored breathing and clenched fists for vibrant living when we discover and appropriately use our God-given gifts.

A Healthy Accountability

If you are a solo artist, you don't especially need accountability. You don't need to keep rhythm with anyone else. You're it—the big cheese.

But when you're using your gifts and doing church as a team, you need to match your stroke to the other members of your team. You need to show up when the schedule tells you to. You need to hang in there when the going gets tough. You can't just quit when the winds pick up. You must be a team player.

Barry Bonds is one of baseball's greatest home-run hitters. So is Babe Ruth. So is Mark McGwire. But what fun would it be if they simply held home-run derbys each week? You buy a ticket and watch pitch after pitch served up as the stars hit as many as they can over the fence. After two hours, the exhibition ends. And next week, you buy another ticket and watch the same thing.

That would get old fast!

These may be great hitters, but outside of playing on a team, they don't light a fire in any fan's heart. Only in the context of a team do they reach their best. There they can contribute their maximum effort and share in the joy of a job well done.

A team keeps us in a healthy accountability with one another. Such a healthy accountability doesn't keep asking, "Did you do this? Did you do that? Come on, fess up!" It doesn't look only for the negative. Healthy accountability sounds more like this: "And let us consider how we may spur one another on toward love and good deeds. Let us not give up meeting together, as some are in the habit of doing, but let us encourage one another—and all the more as you see the Day approaching" (Heb. 10:24-25, *NIV*). The kind of accountability that God encourages us to develop enables us to stay committed to one another and to find our proper place in relationships.

God designed us to work best in teams, not in solo acts. In the Bible, He uses phrases such as, "[we] are Christ's Body, and individually members of it" to remind us of our design (1 Cor. 12:27).

Why is accountability so important? Without accountability, you will never build character. Accountability is one of God's favorite tools for building the character we need. Watch those who have chosen to dodge accountability. They look good in the calm, but when the storm hits, they are no match for the stresses and currents—and before too long, they capsize. Character is the inner strength that carries you to the finish. Character is the stabilizing weight beneath the surface. And character forms best with others around.

Michael Plant was one of the world's best yachtsmen. Many times he navigated the Pacific Ocean as a solo voyager. Through those experiences Plant gained both skill and notoriety. In 1992, he decided to try a new challenge.

He purchased a state-of-the-art sailboat with the best navigational equipment money could buy. He christened his dreamboat *The Coyote*. This boat featured an emergency global positioning locator that, with one press of a button, would transmit a signal designed to be picked up by satellite. Within a few seconds, either of two ground locations could pinpoint Plant's coordinates, even in the middle of the vast ocean. *The Coyote* was the most fail-safe vessel of its kind.

Early in the fall of 1992, Plant set out from the East Coast on a solo voyage—destination, France. On the fourth day of the trip, ground locators lost contact with *The Coyote*. Weather scans of the Atlantic showed storms causing high seas, and it was assumed that Plant was navigating around the storms and would soon regain contact.

He never did.

Search-and-rescue squads scurried to the last known location of *The Coyote*, but to no avail. Commercial airline pilots were asked to monitor their emergency channels in case Plant tried to broadcast signals for help.

Two weeks after his departure, a ship about 400 miles off the Azores came upon *The Coyote*, floating upside down. If there's one position where a state-of-the-art global positioning locator will not be of much use, it's upside down.

Hoisting *The Coyote* up for a closer look, the rescuers searched the cabin, hoping to find the emergency life raft already deployed, which would indicate that Michael Plant might still be alive and floating somewhere in the Atlantic. But they found the life raft only partially inflated, still stuck in the hull of the boat. To this day, the body of Michael Plant has not been found.

A broken keel turned out to be the telltale culprit in the accident. No one knows whether *The Coyote* hit some ocean sewage, a submarine or a whale, but the ballast had been broken off, leaving the boat without any weight in her keel. The ballast, an 8,000-pound weight, made this sailboat one of the safest vessels on the ocean. Even should it capsize, the ballast would force her to roll upright again. Without the ballast, however, *The Coyote* was no match for the Atlantic's fierce storms.

I don't know much about sailing, but one thing I do know: To have stability in a storm, there must be *more weight beneath the waterline than above it.* Without ballast, a boat can look fine in the harbor. Its sails may unfurl majestically and its colors fly, but without any weight in its keel, the boat cannot safely launch out into the deep. And as the old saying goes, Ships are safe in the harbor, but that's not what ships were made for.

Character is the weight beneath our waterline. Without it, we may look good in the harbor. We may strut our accomplishments and display our trophies, but difficult tests just around the corner will surely cause us to capsize.

Storms may not develop character, but they certainly *reveal* it. Only genuine accountability will build the character we need. And the best accountability available comes in teams.

Accelerated Growth

God designed us to make use of our gifts. He created us to serve, anointed us to serve and gifted us to serve. That's God's plan. In fact, using our gifts in service is a crucial and indispensable ingredient for spiritual growth. It's all part of the package.

One year, we took a tour to Israel. I loved our stop at the Dead Sea. It's a beautiful, expansive lake, touching Jordan's borders on its eastern shore and Israel in the west. The abundant mineral deposits of the Dead Sea make it one of the richest spots on earth. Normal seawater contains about 4 percent mineral content, giving it a salty taste. The Dead Sea, by contrast, has a mineral content of *22 percent!* Scattered throughout the lake you can see pillars of salt reaching toward the surface, like lone soldiers awaiting a command that never comes. The water, which looks more like baby oil than it does ocean water, lazily laps the shores.

As beautiful and rich as the Dead Sea is, you won't see any of the familiar sights common around Middle Eastern lakes. You'll find no fishing villages, no boats, no drying nets, no villagers haggling over fish prices or sea gulls gliding overhead. Why not? Because nothing lives in the Dead Sea—hence, its name. *Dead.* The heavy mineral content makes the water uninhabitable for fish or any of other living creatures common to nearby lakes, such as the Sea of Galilee. The Dead Sea is rich but dead—abundant and wealthy, but lifeless.

The main reason for the total absence of life? It has no outlet. For eons, the headwaters of the Jordan have fed this lake, freely depositing their enormous mineral treasures. But because the Dead Sea is a cul-de-sac in a desert located nearly 1,200 feet below sea level, it can release its intake of water only through evaporation. It has no currents of water, no flowing tributaries and no traces of life on its shores.

Churches can likewise turn into dead seas, rich in content but lifeless. Only one thing can get the life process flowing again, and that's to open up an outlet. We have to get our gifts moving and our hearts serving, and then the currents of life will reappear.

Every congregation runs the risk of entropy and stagnation. A church can look good from afar but, like the fig tree described in Mark 11:12-14, up close may reveal a scarcity of fruit. Using our gifts to do church as a team is a nonnegotiable part of growth.

People are like sponges. Put a sponge under a faucet of running water and what happens? It soon becomes saturated. Once that happens, you can run the water over it all day, but it can't absorb any more water. The only way to restore the sponge's absorbency is to wring it out.

As Christians, we absorb teaching, instruction and wisdom

from God's Word; but at some point, if we refuse to serve, we stop growing. Why? We get saturated and lose our capacity to absorb. No matter how many more messages we hear, we can absorb no more truth until we wring out our sponges. Then, and only then, will our absorbency return.

Wring out your sponge and serve! Don't hang on to the water. Give it away freely. There's plenty more where that came from.

In high school I was a novice guitar player. I would add about one new chord a month to my repertoire—a slow boat to guitar proficiency, but I figured that slow and steady was better than no launch at all. I would dream about playing in a band, performing for school dances and proms, but at my usual pace, I calculated that it would take me another 170 years before I'd be ready to perform in public.

Nevertheless, my big chance came at the end of my junior year. Just before summer break, the lead guitarist of the top band in our school approached me, looking for a rhythm guitarist and lead vocalist. He asked if I would consider joining them. His request flabbergasted me! This was my dream come true. Of course, I said yes.

Only one catch: The band's summer schedule started in three weeks, and I had to learn 20 new songs. We would practice three times a week until we got the new songs down.

I felt so excited, I couldn't sleep at night. I sang those songs over and over until I memorized every word, every move and every chord. Each waking moment I dedicated to learning. I can't even remember whether I passed my finals that year (I suppose I must have, since they let me go). I do remember that before I joined a band, I had, at best, minimal growth rate on the guitar. But as soon as I joined the band, my growth accelerated at least 200 percent. I learned chords I didn't even know existed.

I had boundless energy and looked forward to playing guitar at every opportunity.

When you get involved in your church by using your gifts, your spiritual growth will accelerate to warp speed. God designed us that way. Don't head for the grandstands when you enter the kingdom of God. Head for the playing field. That's where the excitement is. That's where the action is.

But most importantly, that's where our Coach is!

Deserving of Our Best

At New Hope we believe that God is worthy of our very best. We have coined a saying around the church: "Simplicity with Excellence." Because we do everything for an audience of One, everything matters. Whether we're cleaning a table or rolling up a microphone cord, God does not deserve our leftovers. He deserves the best we can give.

Excellence is very different from perfection or opulence, things the Lord does not expect of us. A spirit of excellence, a quality found in the life of Daniel (see Dan. 1:17-20; 5:12; 6:3), urges us on to give God our first fruits—our very best in all we do, because we are serving the King of kings.

Some years ago, a clothing store called me to ask if I would pick up a few boxes that it wanted to donate to a worthy cause. The manager said that one of his bosses from corporate head-quarters was coming in and he needed to spruce up the place, and the boxes were in the way. Our director of Mercy Ministries and I had just been talking about setting up a thrift store in our church, so the invitation really excited me. Maybe they would have enough clothing to get the thrift store started!

When I arrived at the store, the manager gave me two large boxes to load into my car. I didn't even ask about the contents.

Grateful for the donation, I thanked him and left.

As soon as I arrived home, I opened the boxes to see if they might contain enough to enable us to begin our new ministry. To my surprise and disappointment, the boxes held nothing I had expected or hoped for. Instead they were filled with broken, soiled and returned items that the store deemed beyond repair: broken purses, mismatched earrings, torn clothing, pants with broken zippers and scratched sunglasses. My heart sank! Every item had been returned to the store because of some serious defect. The store had thrown these items into boxes and hidden them away in some forgotten corner until the management needed to dispose of them. They had decided these items could go either to the dump or to the church. This time, I guess, the church "won."

I did what I could to repair the few salvageable items and disposed of the rest. I felt amused when, two days later, the manager called and asked for a tax-deductible receipt.

After musing over these things, I came to a gripping thought. *Where did they learn this? Who taught them that if they had a choice between trashing something or giving it to God, that it would be a nice, benevolent thing to let God have it?*

And then it hit me: *We have taught them those lessons!*

Over the years, we Christians have modeled this behavior quite effectively. We clean out our closets once a year, and if we find old sweaters with holes in them, pants that don't fit or things we can't use anymore, we give those things to the church.

But God deserves the very first of our hearts, not our last!

When you worship, worship Him with everything that is within you.

When you serve, serve Him with all you've got.

If you sing, sing your heart out.

Train, don't just try. Prepare, don't just perform. Practice, don't just pray. Do both, and in doing so, you will be giving God your best.

Remember, *everything* matters because He deserves our everything!

Team Preparation

1. Why do you think accountability is so difficult for some people?
2. What would be the hardest tests of accountability for you? Why?
3. Read Daniel 5:12. Daniel is said to have possessed an "extraordinary spirit." Some translations call it a "spirit of excellence." Name some characteristics of this kind of spirit.

Notes
1. Mother Teresa, Georges Gorrée and Jean Barbier, *The Love of Christ: Spiritual Counsels* (San Francisco: Harper and Row, 1982), n.p.
2. Norman Cousins, *Anatomy of an Illness* (New York: Bantam Doubleday Dell, 1991), n.p.

C h a p t e r   7

MINING LEADERSHIP GIFTS IN THE CHURCH

Their leader will be one of their own; their ruler
will arise from among them.
JEREMIAH 30:21, *NIV*

One of the most critical keys to doing church as a team is to build an ever-increasing core of servant-leaders. No pastor was designed to do church alone.

Imagine that I hold out before you a one-square-inch piece of cardboard, and on it I slowly empty a bucket of white sand. As the grains accumulate, a small pyramid of sand forms. Soon it will overflow the edges of the cardboard and cascade onto the floor. Now, what will happen if I pour a second bucket of sand onto the cardboard? Will it hold any more? Obviously not! And what if I empty a third bucket of sand onto it? It still refuses to hold any more. (But the floor is certainly a mess.) What do we have to do to hold more sand?

We have to increase the base.

The leadership in any church can be likened to that piece of cardboard. The larger the base, the more "sand" it can hold. If your leadership base is small, it doesn't matter how much sand you pour, it will be impossible for you to hold any more sand until you increase the size of the base!

That's the secret to what many churches call "closing the back door." Some church leaders feel as if their doors are turnstiles through which people come in but never stay. Visitors can't seem to become part of the life of the church, so they leave. Increasing the leadership base by building a solid core of willing servants is primary to a church's foundation for the future.

Finding by Believing!

But where do you find all these wonderful, potential leaders? Do they just appear? "Ours," you may say, "seem to vaporize." Churches often complain that they have a hard time finding good leaders. Many seem to come up with the same reasoning for their unsuccessful churches: "We don't have any leaders!"

So where to start?

The first step in building a core of leaders is to *believe that they are there.* You must believe that God would never call a leader to oversee a ministry without providing everything that the ministry needs to become fruitful and successful. God is not so cruel as to call you to build an ark without providing the necessary materials for its construction. God is not so disorganized as to request a ministry and then forget to supply what it needs!

God will always provide everything you need to fulfill what He has called you to do. But first you must believe that the leaders are there. Why? Because they are! Look for them. See them. They might be right under your nose; but if you are not looking for them, you'll never see them.

If I am looking for my shoes, but I don't believe they are in the closet, then I won't look there. Likewise, if I don't believe there are great potential leaders in my church, then I won't look there to find them.

So look!

God Has Already Provided

Exodus 15:22-26 describes the children of Israel voicing the first of many complaints after being delivered from bondage in Egypt. They had crossed the Red Sea and traveled inland until they ran out of water.

The hot sands of the Sinai have baked the Israelites until they feel parched and thirsty. After a few miles, they come upon a small lake, but the water tastes bitter and unfit to drink. Like the bitterness of the lake, feelings of anger expressed in grumbling and disgust get unleashed against Moses and Aaron. "What shall we drink?" the people demand. Then Scripture gives us a beautiful gem for every leader:

> Then he cried out to the LORD, and the LORD *showed him*
> *a tree*; and he threw it into the waters, and the waters
> became sweet (Exod. 15:25, emphasis added).

Moses cried out to the Lord, and when he did so, God showed him a tree. If you read this portion again, you will discover that God didn't create a tree for Moses. God didn't transplant a tree. He didn't cause a tree to appear. In fact, the tree had always been there; God just showed him the tree.

Moses and Aaron must have walked by that tree dozens of times without once recognizing its potential. The people may have grumbled while eating lunch under that tree. The people complained because it didn't seem as though God had provided an answer to their dilemma of extreme thirst, desert heat and a sour lake. Yet all the while, the answer to their plight sat right under their noses! (Or, rather, right above their heads.) Because they were too busy complaining about what they didn't have, their eyes remained blind to what they did have.

So many of God's people through the ages became so preoccupied with what God had not provided for them that they remained oblivious to the wondrous gifts He had given them.

Let God show you the tree. It's there, and so are your leaders. In fact, maybe you're scheduled to have lunch with them this week! You may be fellowshipping with them today—but you will never be able to see them until you believe that they are there.

You Gotta See the Houses in the Forest

A dear pastor friend and I were talking over lunch one day. He was having trouble finding quality leaders in his church and he seemed on the verge of burnout from undertaking many of the ministry responsibilities himself.

"If I had a bigger church," he observed, "there would be more leaders to choose from. But right now there just aren't any!"

"Sure there are," I replied "You just have to see them."

"No," he countered. "You have leaders because you have a

large church. Mine is small, so I don't have any leaders."

I pushed back, admittedly with a slight tone of frustration in my voice: "When you look at a forest, what do you see?"

"Elementary, Watson," he quipped. "Trees!"

"That's your problem," I replied. "All you see are trees."

I could tell that he wasn't quite tracking with me.

"Let me explain," I continued. "When I look at a forest, I see houses. I see beautiful dressers, rocking chairs, bed frames, cabinets and desks. They're all in the forest, and they're beautiful."

From the look on his face, I could see that he was beginning to question the benefit of our having lunch together. I could almost read his thoughts: *Your forests in Hawaii must be a lot different from ours, 'cause all we got are trees!*

Before he could jump to any premature conclusions, I hastened to my point.

"No, you won't find them already completed. But the potential is all there! Sure, you'll still have to cut and sand and varnish the wood, but it's all there. Everything you need to furnish your entire home is in that forest. You just need to see more than trees in order to be motivated to harvest the wood. You have to see their potential. You gotta believe there's gold in them thar hills if you're gonna muster up the energy you need to mine it out."

Here's the absolute truth: When you really believe that leaders are there, you'll be surprised at how many wonderful leaders start showing up.

Building a Leadership Base

Still, you have to make it as easy as possible for those leaders to start showing up. That's why every healthy church culture works to provide an easy entrance into significant involvement. Too often, only the well oriented and the veterans know the way. Doing church as a team opens the portals and lowers the threshold.

One piece of advice has kept me from many unnecessary pains: "Don't hire those who can do it well. Hire those who can facilitate others who will do it well."

In other words, hire only those who understand this: "You will have the privilege of doing ministry, but with one stipulation: You have to do it THROUGH another person!"

Some years ago, when we began New Hope, one leader became more and more adept at computers in our office. As we continued to grow, so did our need for increased computer technology and computer maintenance. We had one volunteer who excelled in this area, and we felt so thankful for his expertise—until one day, I realized that if we ever had a problem, we were up a creek without a paddle.

And then that day came.

This man began to offer his services to us at a price, but soon the price increased until we found ourselves painted into a corner. No one knew what to do except him. He kept everything a secret, which he felt gave him job security. As soon as I realized what was going on, I gave him a new adventure in the exciting field of job hunting.

From then on, I remained much more vigilance and took pains to make sure that we all understood that none of us is indispensable, including me. We had to have enough trust in Jesus to open the entrance and include others in increasing ways.

We instructed our sound ministry to label all the necessary switches on each soundboard so that anyone would know how to turn it on or off.

Cartons get labeled and teams are periodically checked to ensure that the base of those "in the know" is steadily increasing.

If you want to find and develop leaders who already come to

your church, you have to do something similar. If you maintain a "closed club," then don't feel surprised when your exhaustion starts causing you to fall asleep on the job.

Ask yourself, *What can I do to open wide our leadership doors? How can I pave the way for an influx of the new leaders we need? Where can I start to make it easier for people to join us, get on board, and take the reins?*

May I make a suggestion? Start with their dreams.

Let It Fly Freely

I lived in Japan during my junior high school years. My father served in the United States Army, and for three years he was stationed in a small town called Zama. We lived in a beautiful place, but it was still an Army installation enclosed by barbed wire. The base looked like any vintage American town, but outside the fences lay the mystique of Japan. I looked forward to our trips off base and into the countryside.

One summer day, all of us kids jumped into the car for a ride into the cool mountains surrounding Tokyo. We stopped at a lookout point that offered a breathtaking view of one of the lush valleys below. Cedar trees blanketed the mountains, and the valleys stretched as far as we could see, each one reaching out to a sleepy village.

We decided to stop for lunch. On one side of the road, a little Japanese woman was selling *bentos*, Japanese box lunches. On the other side, a man dressed in a traditional *yukata*, or "happy coat," caught my attention. He was selling tiny birds. He held a dozen or so bamboo cages, each one containing a small bird that resembled a finch.

"*Irrashai-mase!*" he called. "Welcome! May I help you?"

"How much for one bird?" I asked.

"100 yen each," he called back in Japanese.

In those days, 100 yen was worth about 36 cents. Such a deal! I handed the vendor a 100-yen coin and selected one of the bamboo cages containing a tiny finch. As I began to walk back to the car to show off my new purchase, the man called out after me.

"*Sumimasen!* [Excuse me!]" he called. "Don't forget to bring the cage back when you're done!"

"Bring back the cage?" I asked with obvious confusion. "I'm not planning to eat the thing. It's going to become my new pet! Besides, without a cage, how do you expect me to get it home?"

"Oh," he replied. "You don't understand. The bird is not for you to take home. You take the bird to the edge of the lookout and release it so it can fly freely!"

Quite frankly, that was about the dumbest thing I had ever heard. I had just paid good money for this bird, and I wasn't about to let it go. But his eyes remained fixed on me, silently soliciting my agreement. I stood there, momentarily hoping for any possible reprieve.

On one hand, I could make a run for it. I knew my sneakers and feet could outrun his *gettas* and socks. But then again, there could be a hidden samurai move or two under his *yukatta*—maybe he'd throw one of those ninja stars at me. So, I figured I'd better comply.

Feeling a little like a pirate who had just surrendered in battle, I politely nodded. I made my way toward the ridge until I felt the cool wind scented with a fresh cedar fragrance brush my face. Before me a cliff dropped dramatically about 50 feet into the lush valley far below.

I gave a final glance at the vendor-turned-sentry (who still had me under his careful surveillance). Out of options, I slowly opened the cage door that separated the bird from its freedom. I tapped on the opposite side of the cage, and the tiny finch hopped its way suspiciously toward the opening. After I prodded it with a final tap on its bamboo prison, it suddenly launched into flight with a jubilant chorus of tweets and whistles. I watched it as it darted over the treetops. It paused momentarily, and then almost as an afterthought, it circled back toward me. It fluttered, hovering briefly as if to say "thank you" to its liberator, then shot up so high that I lost him in the sun.

I stood there transfixed, suspended in a moment of fresh discovery. I had never experienced such a feeling. I couldn't put my finger on it, but I knew something inside me had changed. I had been captured by an unforeseen lesson that would forever alter my life.

I walked slowly back toward the emancipator of birds. I returned the empty cage and he bowed in the traditional form. With the reverent posture of a young disciple before his sensei, I returned the gesture, my skepticism replaced by the sobering humility of a lesson well learned.

I didn't return home with a newfound pet, but rather with something much more profound. This lesson has accompanied me throughout the years, forever changing my perspective about serving people. Looking back now, I would have paid a hundred times more if I had even a hint of the life-changing power of that one experience. I learned the lesson of what it means to become a *Dream Releaser*.

I believe that in every person's heart lives a dream of what they can be for God. Our churches are filled with these untapped gold mines, many of them potential leaders. Each dream, if released, can unleash a person's destiny and God-given calling. But often, these dreams go undetected and unfulfilled—and that's why so many of us have such trouble finding effective leaders.

"Tell 'Em I Died Rich"

Two miners spent half their lives looking for gold in the Pacific Northwest. Despite the mocking criticism of the townspeople, the two miners pressed on, believing in their ability to strike it rich. The pair soon became the joke of the town, as week after week, they returned from their labors empty-handed. Nevertheless, they pressed on with a deep confidence that *someday* they would find what they were looking for.

One sultry afternoon, after months of painstaking work in an old mine shaft, they finally hit pay dirt. One moment, they saw only rock; the next, they glimpsed huge nuggets of gold shining out of the darkness from a rich, undiscovered vein. With furious abandon the men began pulling nugget after nugget from the grip of the earth.

No one knows whether it was a faulty support pole, the exuberance of the shouting or the gradual loosening of the dirt that caused the collapse, but soon the sound of loud, piercing cracks in the timber brought the two men to an abrupt halt. Suddenly the mineshaft caved in, and tons of falling dirt pounded both men to the floor.

One of the men lay injured on the ground, holding tightly to a nugget he had just claimed. The other miner, still able to move, pulled himself up, yelling, "Come on! We've got to get out of here before the whole thing collapses! I'll help you. Get up! Leave the gold. We don't have a second to lose!"

The injured miner, still clutching the gold nugget tightly to his chest, said, "No. Just leave me here. I found what I've been looking for. I've spent my life searching for this vein, and I'm not about to let it go now. Leave me here. You go! Get out of here."

"Don't be foolish! We've gotta get you back!" his partner replied. Just then, the rafters trembled again, spilling more dirt into the dust-filled shaft.

"If I leave you here, you'll surely die! What will I tell your family? What will I tell the folks back in town?"

The badly injured miner wheezed his final words between strained coughs, as dust filled the collapsing chamber.

"Just tell 'em I died rich," he whispered with a final breath. "Just tell 'em I died rich."

Dream Releasers

The church—yours included—is laden with treasures, dreams and precious gifts. Yet too many precious souls go to their graves with songs unsung, gifts tightly wrapped and dreams unreleased. Too many of God's people are dying rich!

> *There is nothing more spectacular than seeing people's dreams released and being used for the glory of God.*

Like the Japanese finch, treasures and dreams need to be released. In every person's heart lives a dream of what he or she can become for the Lord—how a person can make a difference in the world, in their family and in their church. The potential leaders in your church have their own dreams, and by helping them see what they are and working with them to give shape to those dreams, you also help to solve your leadership shortage.

God calls all of us, and especially every leader, to become a Dream Releaser. There is nothing more spectacular than seeing people's dreams released and being used for the glory of God. There's just no greater joy.

That's just what the founder of Youth With A Mission, Loren Cunningham, did. He released the dreams in the hearts of thousands of young people to go into the mission fields, and their dreams came to pass. Through his vision and leadership, Loren mobilized scores of young evangelists who today continue to bring the good news to unreached people groups.

Mother Teresa did the same in Calcutta. God had deposited the gifts of mercy and servanthood into the hearts of thousands of willing servants, but before Mother Teresa entered the scene, those gifts lay dormant. She found a way for those dreams to be discovered and then developed and deployed to reach the poorest of the poor in Calcutta. What's more, she developed leaders where none had existed before.

We all have dreams in our hearts just waiting to be released. These gifts, if mobilized and aligned toward a common, God-glorifying purpose, can transform any congregation into a powerful army for the Lord.

More often than not, the potential that lies within our hearts gets covered over by fear and immaturity, character flaws and insecurities. We need someone to believe in us, to mentor and disciple us through the uncertainties. We need genuine words of encouragement that prompt us to higher heights. We need leaders who will nurture leaders.

Such was the case in my life. One person with an ability to steward the power of words changed my life. Her name was Grace Flint. In the book *The Dream Releasers*, I tell her story.

When I received Christ, I was 19, and set on fire! I felt the unmistakable call to enter full-time ministry. Three months later, I headed for Bible college. One of the Campus Crusade counselors had given me a paperback *Living New Testament* the day I became a Christian. With my trusty paperback and John 3:16 memorized, I was armed and dangerous. I enrolled high on zeal and low on knowledge.

I remember well the first day of class. The teacher introduced a short devotional by saying, "Let's all turn to Jeremiah."

Now, I had no idea who Jeremiah was. Ready to meet what I thought was a new student, I spun my chair around to give attention to whoever Jeremiah was. From the snickering of the other students, I knew something was amiss.

"In your Bible, Wayne. Turn to Jeremiah . . . in your Bible!" came a condescending voice from a smug kid sitting next to me.

Well, that didn't help much. I spent the whole period looking for Jeremiah in the New Testament. I sighed with relief when the class ended, leaving me quite embarrassed and questioning my readiness for the school year ahead of me.

The next class, however, would be different. It was Bible History taught by Dr. Grace Flint. She was a brilliant scholar, but it wasn't her scholarship that I remember most.

I remember her as a Dream Releaser.

She was tough as nails. Our homework assignments could not be turned in handwritten; they had to be typed. Computers were scarce in the early '70s. No Macs, no Dells, and no Compaq laptops. The only thing IBM had to offer was an electric typewriter (the delete key being a tube of whiteout).

I recall getting my first assignment returned by Sister Flint (as we respectfully addressed our female instructors). The grade was noticeably missing, but in its place was a handwritten note:

Thank you for being in my class, Wayne. Your insight and contribution was so refreshing during the discussion we had. Your obvious zeal for Christ inspires us all. I look with great anticipation for how God will use you for His purposes. *The Kingdom of God awaits you!*

I felt so inspired! I must have read and reread that last line a dozen times before lights out that evening. The following day, I couldn't wait for her class to begin. I took every class she taught, not so much because I liked Bible history, but because I so desperately needed the words of a Dream Releaser. Like a wandering desert Bedouin, I would drink deeply of the fresh waters that her words provided. On every paper she would scribble a handwritten note that would gradually unlock my potential.

It was her way of saying, "I believe in you" that tapped my cage and nudged my dreams into flight.

Churches that function well overflow with dream releasers. Dream Releasers set the culture; they develop the kind of atmosphere where young, emerging leaders thrive. They create an environment where serving becomes a delight rather than a chore. In a dream releasing church, hearts, as well as dreams, tend to soar.

Security Checkpoint

Dream Releasers who set the environment for doing church as a team must have one outstanding quality: *security*. Pastors and leaders, if you do not feel secure as a leader, you will find it virtually impossible to attract, develop or retain others. You cannot do church as a team while battling insecurity.

Good leaders must be able to build confidence in others. If you feel easily intimidated by other leaders and find it hard to rejoice and congratulate others who excel above you, then probably you suffer from insecurity.

King Saul's insecurity showed most clearly in his violent intimidation of David. This anxious and fearful king's *modus operandi* employed sabotage, slander and continual efforts to discredit the young leader. Saul's insecurity became his arch nemesis. If Saul had been a Dream Releaser instead of a dream killer, he still would be venerated as one of the world's greatest mentors. Instead, if we remember him at all, we recall him as that "loser" who preceded King David.

Secure people encourage others and enjoy their successes. They can appreciate and applaud the achievements of those whom they have put into key positions. Secure leaders are neither territorial nor possessive. They willingly, even eagerly, surround themselves with people more qualified than themselves.

Insecure people, on the other hand, feel that if they do not control everything around them, then they are not doing their job. They fear criticism and they worry about what others think. Insecure leaders cannot tolerate it when others outperform them. In fact, insecure leaders tend to sabotage the successes of others in order to protect themselves. Hence, they *use* people, but seldom do they *develop* people.

Take a look at yourself as a leader. You will do well if you can catch people doing things *right* and show genuine excitement for their accomplishments. You might be surprised at how much can get accomplished when we don't care who gets the credit!

Take a look at this checklist and see how you fare:

A secure leader	An insecure leader
Encourages others' attempts	Sabotages others' efforts
Points out others' strong points	Brings attention to others' faults
Overlooks flaws	Uses others' flaws as ammunition
Readily admits own mistakes	Is defensive and justifies mistakes
Gives away credit to others	Demands or manipulates credit
Rejoices when others succeed	Feels jealous of others' successes
Is excited when others do it better	Is easily intimidated
Is willing to risk to improve	Plays it safe to retain position
Is content to remain anonymous	Requires others to notice
Is quick to build teams	Wants to do things himself
Can take time off	Can't allow others to rise up and lead

What kind of leader are you? How did you score? Are you some-one who enjoys it when others succeed? Can you easily give cred-it away and show genuine excitement at the accomplishments of others? How hard is it for you to build a team and give away credit?

Ask yourself one final question: If you're having trouble locating effective leaders in your church, could it be that you don't really *want* to find them?

Reaching for Success

As you build your team, make sure you work hard to include new people, and don't allow yourself to feel intimidated when others do it better than you. God will always have a place for you, and the greater a servant you are, the greater the joy you'll experience.

If your gift is to build platforms for other emerging leaders, then when they succeed, God will call you to build more. You might not be worth two cents as a carpenter of wood or a mason of stone, but if you can use human potential to build emerging leaders, then you'll leave a legacy of awesome con-struction that will continue to shape the world long after you're gone.

And how can you be any more "successful" than that?

Team Preparation

1. List two dreams tucked away in your heart that have yet to come true.

   a.

   b.

2. What factors hinder each dream from coming to pass?

   a.

   b.

   c.

3. Make a list of four people who would make good leaders in any church if they were slotted into ministry correctly.

4. Name several reasons we fail to see the potential in others.

DEVELOPING SERVANT-LEADERS

*Give me one hundred preachers who fear nothing but sin
and desire nothing but God, and I care not a straw whether they
be clergymen or laymen, such alone will shake the gates of
hell and set up the kingdom of God upon earth.*

JOHN WESLEY, 1703–1791

A pastor has few greater roles than to believe in the people under his care. This lone quality can do more to develop emerging leaders in a church than any class or group study.

We all need someone to believe in us—someone who will see the best in us and help us to bring it forth. Sure, we may have many faults that still need to be corrected, but even more we need people who will look beyond our glitches to see God's best.

Reuben Gets a Lesson

Jesus modeled for us how to fertilize the soil of human hearts so that ordinary men and women can grow into wonderful servants. He did this in an especially memorable way in a remarkable episode recounted in Mark 2.

The story opens with four zealous friends of a paralytic we'll call Reuben. The friends hear that a wonder-working carpenter from Nazareth is teaching at Peter's house in Capernaum.

Now, a visiting teacher is not all that unique. Guest rabbis often taught in the neighborhood synagogues. But what catches the attention of these four friends are the many reports of Jesus healing sick and hurting people, and they can't help but think of their friend Reuben.

That evening, with their friend lying on a stretcher, they begin their journey to Peter's house. The heavy and awkward load delays their arrival, however, and by the time they reach the home, a crowd has filled the living room and overflowed into the backyard, leaving no room for latecomers.

Refusing to let their hopes die, the most creative among them comes up with a risky idea. "I know what we can do!" he says. "Let's climb up on the roof and make a hole! You heard me. Make a hole! Then we can let Reuben down on the stretcher right in front of this teacher. That'll get His attention, won't it?" Without wasting any time, the four friends clamber onto the roof with ol' Reuben in tow and proceed to execute Plan A with a passion.

They work with such urgency that they don't stop even to calculate the repair bill for Peter's roof. Had they known the reputation of this rough fisherman and of his volatile outbursts, I doubt they would have carried out their scheme. But they were in too much of a hurry to worry about such details.

After another burst of team energy, poor Reuben lies helplessly dangling in front of the guest speaker. Above him, four pairs of eyes curiously gaze through the newly crafted skylight. The room falls into an uncomfortable silence as everyone holds their breath, awaiting the reprimand of the Master. After all, what would the scribes think? What would the Law demand? Would the Teacher chide the zealous, unthinking friends? Would He demand they immediately undertake repairs to Peter's roof?

Jesus' response holds for us a leadership principle worth a pound of gold. Instead of chastising the zealous friends for their ill-planned exploit, He fixes His gaze on them. The Bible captures the moment with these words:

> And Jesus *seeing their faith* said to the paralytic, "My son, your sins are forgiven" (Mark 2:5, emphasis added).

Jesus could have chided Reuben's friends for their extreme measures or lack of preplanning. He could have pointed out their tardiness, due either to their procrastination or late departure. Instead, He saw their *faith!* He saw the action of Reuben's friends for what it was—and he defined it as faith.

A Leader Looks for the Best

Look for faith in those around you and you will begin to see more instances of faith. Look for evidence of God's presence, not evidence of His absence. In each of us throbs a desire for God's best. Every person has a yearning to do well, to make a difference. God created us that way!

Take special note of young entrepreneurs and their novice attempts to fly. Sometimes those attempts look more like a disoriented albatross than the takeoff of an F-22 fighter jet. No matter. Encourage them, even if the plane fails to make it off the tarmac. See the faith and the heart behind their attempt. While the execution of their dreams may require further development, the potential inside each of them is a precious commodity to God.

Sure, they will need some recalibrating and adjustments—but when you begin to see people through the eyes of Jesus, watch what happens! You'll begin to see miracles multiply and a corresponding decrease in justifications for why nothing remarkable seems to be happening in your church.

Some of the greatest discoveries occur when people readjust their eyes to see what's best about a situation rather than what's worst.

One afternoon when George De Mestral went walking his dog, the dog got loose and ran off through some tall grass. When George finally retrieved his wayward pet, the canine was covered with burrs, all tangled in his fur. When George arrived home, he could have cursed the dog while cutting the burrs out. Instead, he got curious. He took a cutting of the fur and viewed it under his microscope. Amazed at the gripping ability of the burrs, he studied them further. George's curiosity and his willingness to see the potential in a sticky situation ultimately led him to invent Velcro!

Controlled Explosions

Positive thinking and creative effort helps to develop young leaders, but you also have to take steps to reduce any possible collateral damage.

Some years ago, we went through a construction program

for a new building. Having purchased raw, undeveloped land, we had much to do. One hefty project included blasting through layers of solid rock in order to allow the land to "drain."

Dynamite was used to minimize shrapnel, and the contractor placed a load of about 100 old vehicle tires over ground zero. He tied them together with wire to reduce the number of unidentified flying objects. During each explosion, the tires would lift into the air a few feet, then come crashing down with the rubbery force of a 250-pound wrestler pinning a lightweight to the mat in a high school match.

New leaders need to work under the supervision and protection of a more veteran overseer. The major difference between a veteran leader and an acolyte is that the newbie has hundreds of mistakes in him or her just waiting to be made. But with the oversight of a veteran, combined with appropriate accountability, you can minimize any explosions and reduce the body count.

At New Hope, we ask each young leader to shadow a more veteran leader. Accountability is crucial, and we constantly check hearts so that no one goes off on his own without his team. "Heart checks" must become a common practice in doing church as a team. Otherwise, the lack of accountability invites shrapnel to fill the air and damage young and old recruits alike. Much better to take careful steps to reduce any collateral damage!

A Personal Responsibility

Let me make a disclaimer here. *As wonderful as it is to have someone who believes in me, in the final analysis, it is my own responsibility to develop my own gifts.* Jesus gave us some clear teaching on investing what God has entrusted to us:

And the one also who had received the one talent came
up and said, "Master, I knew you to be a hard man. . . .
I was afraid, and went away and hid your talent in the
ground; see, you have what is yours." But his master
answered and said to him, "You wicked, lazy slave, you
knew that I reap where I did not sow, and gather where I
scattered no seed. Then you ought to have put my
money in the bank, and on my arrival I would have
received my money back with interest. Therefore take
away the talent from him, and give it to the one who has
the ten talents. For to everyone who has shall more be
given, and he shall have an abundance; but from the one
who does not have, even what he does have shall be
taken away" (Matt. 25:24-29).

I have heard many applications of this story, but one central
message rings with special power: *You can't please God by not investing!* We must use our gifts, not bury them. I would rather risk all
for God and come up short than never make the attempt at all.

Leaders develop their gifts by taking risks for God. If everything were a guaranteed success, then why would we ever need
faith? We do need it, however, for the Bible tells us, "Without
faith, it is impossible to please [God]" (Heb. 11:6). We cannot
please God by playing it safe.

Are you willing to risk what you have for the sake of the
Master? Too many of us allow our fear to control us, so we bury
our gifts and then wonder why we never grow or increase in our
giftedness and influence. One key to the success of the Early
Church was that these men and women "risked their lives for the
name of our Lord Jesus Christ" (Acts 15:26).

One of my favorite Bible verses is Proverbs 14:4: "Where no
oxen are, the manger is clean, but much increase comes by the

strength of the ox." In other words, strength always brings problems, but that's normal! Don't fear making mistakes. If your goal is to keep a clean manger, then you won't need (or want) any oxen. But if you desire to make a difference with your life, then you need to be ready and willing to clean up a few piles of doodoo.

Risk: The Breakfast of Champions

If you're afraid of messes, if you're afraid of failing, if you're afraid of risking, then you'll never get anywhere. As a baseball player once said, "You can't steal second with your foot still on first." You have to be willing to venture off the bag. So take the lead and go for it!

In Hawaii, we often hear advertisements beckoning potential travelers to Las Vegas for a weekend of gambling. The advertisers offer very reasonable fares and hotel rooms at bargain prices—but of course, they plan to more than make up their losses by luring you to drop your hard-earned dollars at the roulette tables or watch them disappear into one of the many one-armed bandits that line the casinos. Each year, millions flock to these hollow promised lands to risk their savings in hope of striking it rich. Many of us think nothing of taking risks with our money, even though we know we have a far greater chance of returning home empty-handed than we do of returning as a millionaire.

C. T. Studd, a great preacher and missionary of yesteryear, once said, "The gamblers for gold are so many, but the gamblers for God are so few. Where are the gamblers for God?"

We risk our lives each time we fly in an airplane. We take a risk when we invest in a stock. We take a risk when we get married. We take a risk when we buy a house. I think it's high time we take a risk for God! He's so much more worthy (and secure) than any earthly investment.

A little poem reminds me that life is all about taking risks:

There once lived a man who never risked,
He never tried.
He never laughed,
He never cried.
Then one day, when he passed away,
His insurance was denied.
They said since he never really lived,
Then he never really died!

—Anonymous

You can develop your gifts only by using them. Sure, using them may involve risk—the risk of making a mistake, the risk of faltering or stammering if you speak, even the risk of failure. Go for it anyway! Don't associate risk with the fear of failure; associate it with pleasing God.

Don't wait to fully develop your gifts before you put them to use. That just won't happen, because gifts don't ripen like a bunch of bananas in a dark place. Gifts hidden away don't ripen; they rot.

Build Your Character Before Building Your Ministry

As a relatively new Christian, I taught several morning Bible studies to a group of seven or eight men. We often met at restaurants where we would pore over the Scriptures and pour coffee down our throats for an hour or so before going to work. Today

I see that I learned more from teaching than I ever gave out. I think God had me teach those studies, not so much for what would happen *through* me as what would happen *in* me.

You see, God is less interested in what you're *doing* than He is in what you're *becoming*.

As I look back over the years, I recall many times when my involvement in some project had little to do with what I could contribute, but it had a lot do with God building my character. Sometimes the Lord placed me in a position because He knew some crucial things needed to develop inside of me.

When you get involved, God will instill character or virtue in you through the process—perhaps endurance, submission, people skills or positive attitudes. God places you in an environment that you enjoy, and while you remain there, He instills His character and likeness. He places you with others who help to shape you—and some who may sand your edges. But all in all, God uses our involvement to develop character strengths that would never develop apart from serving.

Consider a letter I wrote to my children that I included in a book called *Gems Along the Way*:

Dear Amy, Aaron and Abby,

I saw a lady's four-carat diamond ring the other day. Wow! Was that ever impressive! The diamond must have been worth $50,000! (After considering it for a moment, I felt strongly that such opulence would surely detract from the natural beauty of your mother's hand, so I refrained from buying it.)

Anyway, the woman's gold band was a simple one, with a few smaller diamonds on either side. Holding the diamond in place was a setting that included maybe five or six prongs.

My! I thought. *That setting had better be strong! It's holding on to $50,000!*

Although the setting doesn't get nearly as much attention as the diamond itself, it is equally as important. Any wise jeweler would never put such a precious jewel in a poor or weak setting. If he did, then one small bump and the gem would be lost. The strength and quality of the setting will determine the security and staying power of the gem.

Character is like that setting. God has promised us such wonderful gems! Yet without the basis of character, His promises would be lost or forfeited at the first bump. The Holy Spirit desires to produce character in each of us prior to the setting of the gems. Whether those gems are marriage, an influential position, a ministry, finances or a family, each of these will require character. This is the setting that needs to be developed prior to the placement of the gem.

Strengthen your setting. Build your character. Learn to forgive, to be diligent, to be honest. Learn to stay steady and faithful, to keep commitments, to go by what you know and not necessarily by what you feel.

Here's a simple definition of character that I heard along the way: *Character is the ability to follow through on a worthy decision long after the emotion of making that decision has passed.*

God will refine your metal until it's pure gold. He will shape your character until it's strong and trustworthy. Then when God sees that the setting is ready, He will be faithful to place His very best gems in your life. That's when you'll shine!

Love,

Dad

I have experienced overwhelming feelings on the job that had nothing to do with my placement; they had far more to do with my character development than with my gifts or passion. What we often define as burnout may actually be the result of personality conflicts or a problem with submission to authority. These are character issues that God wants to deal with, once and for all. If we bail out, the lesson will have to be repeated in another setting—second verse, same as the first.

This is where accountability through friendships has become a lifesaver for me. I need people watching out for me, and I need to do the same for others. I urge you to develop relationships along the way that are deep enough to allow these friends to speak into your life. To do church as a team successfully, you have to stay committed to one another's success. If we could do that for each other (you may sing this next line), what a wonderful world this would be!

Take Me Out to the Ball Game!

Character does not develop outside of involvement. It develops "online." It grows only when we begin to apply what God asks of us, even though it may, at times, seem beyond our reach. God gives us gifts in "kit-form," in packages of potential, and we get the privilege of developing that potential into reality. But it will require us to take the risk, to jump in and swing the bat.

Let's say that during a revival campaign you received the gift of . . . well, er . . . the ability to play professional baseball (just for the sake of illustration). Hands were laid on your head, bestowing this rare and wonderful gift upon you. But even though the gift is now yours, you still look the same, act the same and walk the same. So what do you have to do to see this gift in action? What must you do in order for it to blossom and mature?

You have to start playing baseball!

So you put on a uniform and go to the ballpark. You've never swung a bat. The coach steps to the pitcher's mound, and you stride to the plate. He throws the first pitch, and you swing with all your might—and miss it by a mile. But do you quit? No! You dust yourself off and take another pitch.

The coach encourages you. "It's in you! Swing again. I know it's in you!" So you take your stance in the batter's box, and the second pitch comes whizzing by and smacks into the catcher's glove. You didn't even see it go by.

"It's in you," the coach says again. "Swing the bat next time. Swing the bat!"

The third pitch rushes toward the plate. You close your eyes and swing with everything you've got.

KABOOM!

The ball rockets off the sweet spot of your Louisville Slugger and sails into the outfield.

"That's it!" shouts the coach. "I knew you had it in you. Keep it up now. Keep it up!"

As the months go by, you continue training. The balls fly further and further. And when you take the field at shortstop, nothing gets by you. You're turning double plays and then triple plays. You begin to *love* this sport! Every day, you haunt the baseball diamond, fielding grounders or hitting home runs.

Now fast-forward three years. Your reputation as a promising rookie has spread, and a couple of scouts from the Atlanta Braves fly in to see one of your games. They watch you hit, field and run the bases like a pro. In the fourth inning, you turn a spectacular double play, and one scout leans over to the other and remarks, "Now, *that* kid has a gift. He has a gift!"

And he's right—but how did your gift become noticeable? How did it come to its fullness?

You had to actually get out and play baseball.

This principle applies equally to doing church as a team. You must use your gift! Even though you miss a few grounders or drop the occasional pop-up, stay in there. I know it's in you because *God put it there!* When you strike out, get in there and swing again. You may get involved in the set-up team or the follow-up team, not so much because you're the best but because God put you there in order for you to develop into your best.

Say yes more often than you say no. Get involved. If after a while, you find that your piece of the puzzle just doesn't fit, then move to another position—but keep serving! Pretty soon you'll be dazzling them in the field and knocking the ball out of the park, and people will look at you and exclaim, "Wow! You are so gifted! How did that happen?"

And you'll reply, "I just played baseball."

Starting in the Shadows

One of the fastest and easiest ways to start serving is through *shadowing*, a practice I briefly referred to earlier. Shadowing is simply following someone around who has been serving in an area that interests you.

Shadowing is a way of introducing new people into a ministry, and we recommend this approach in almost every volunteer ministry at New Hope. It's a low-risk orientation that gives budding "ministers" a glimpse of what is being done and how. It's also an opportunity for everyone to build new friendships along the way.

Each person who is currently serving in any capacity is instructed to keep an open door for someone to shadow him or her. Then they learn the three stages of the shadowing process:

Stage 1—I do. You watch.

Stage 2—We do together.

Stage 3—You do. I applaud!

A new servant joining the team provides the tipping point of the greatest joy in doing church as a team. It increases the team even as it increases the joy.

Passing Batons

Have you ever wondered why Jesus sent out His disciples two by two? I believe it was because He knew that the gospel could best be seen and understood in the context of relationships. As people witnessed the love, friendship and camaraderie of the two messengers, this gave credence to the message.

> *Passing the baton in ministry isn't meant to be a sudden, last-ditch effort, any more than it is in a relay race.*

As you read through the Gospels, you notice something interesting about the leadership style of Jesus: He began passing batons to His disciples early in His ministry. By the sixth chapter of Mark, He is already choosing a dozen men to succeed Him.

Passing the baton in ministry isn't meant to be a sudden, last-ditch effort, any more than it is in a relay race. Plan on it. Start passing batons early in your ministry. Make "passing batons" a part of team ministry.

When my daughter Amy was a senior in high school, she ran on the relay team in track. I watched as the team practiced one skill again and again. They would all line up, facing the same direction, about an arm's length apart from each other. Then, while running in place, they would practice passing the baton from one runner to the other. When the baton got passed from the back to the front, they repeated the process until they achieved perfect passes. The reason? In a relay, the race is either won or lost in the passing of the baton.

Passing the baton is a function of our willingness to allow others into the joys of serving God. It is an important deterrent to possessiveness and territorialism. A spirit of protectiveness will only wreak havoc and discourage new and emerging leaders.

I urge you to invite others into your area of ministry and then eagerly applaud their successes. Fight the tendency to become protective. An open invitation to get involved is crucial for developing an atmosphere of growth and teamwork. Answering our call and using our gifts includes being led by the Holy Spirit to help others become successful.

Remember, it's not about us. The world does not revolve around you or me. I am His servant and I exist for His purposes, not He for mine. This is part of what it means to do church as a team.

Unlike a relay team, however, you pass batons to *all* the team members. Then you run together! You don't pass a baton and then quit. You stay with the team and you run in unison. I guess this would be better described as "passing *out* batons." When we look at the larger picture of God's plan for the church in a particular community, we can see the crucial place of passing out batons. A team has to run together.

Learn to pass out batons, and do it early. Don't wait until the end.

When I began studying the early missionary efforts to Hawaii, Titus Coan became one of my heroes, as did Hiram Bingham. These men served the people of Hawaii during the early and middle 1800s. While Coan and Bingham did hundreds of things right in reaching the Hawaiian Islands, they also made two costly mistakes that hindered the future of their ministries.

First, they allowed their second generation to be lost—their own children grew up without a deep and genuine faith. While no one reason probably accounts for this mistake, no doubt the missionaries piled their plates so full that they had little time left for their own children. A poignant lesson for us all!

Second, these men erred in passing the baton far too late in life. Just before his death, Titus Coan passed the mantle of leadership to a few potential leaders. They carried on as best they could but, inevitably, the mission shrank and the vision faded.

It may take only a moment to pass a baton, but it takes years to pass the *heart* of that baton. When doing church as a team, passing batons early ensures that no one burns out and that we all share the joys (and sorrows) together. At New Hope, we don't pass batons as a precursor to the end of one's ministry. We *pass batons as a way of including others in the race.*

You don't pass the baton in a relay race once you've pooped out; you pass it at the very apex of your stride. The same is true in doing church as a team. So invite others into your ministry. Don't consider passing batons an exit strategy, but as an invitational one. It is for inclusion and team building, not merely for transition.

Start by Serving Each Other

Although serving the Lord and others is best done in teams, you can encourage this to happen by first serving the others on your team. Some call this *lateral serving*, in which serving one another is given equal importance with serving to get something accomplished. This is the *esprit de corps* of a church.

Lateral serving is the opposite of an attitude that says "That's not my ministry" or "That's not my responsibility." It's a willingness to occasionally do someone else's job and do it with great joy. It is seeing a task overlooked by others and gratefully filling in. I have heard lateral serving described as the art of making good on someone else's mistake.

In doing church as a team, we have learned the importance of cross training—training outside our specialties so that we can step up and step in when others need a break or simply need our support. Everyone has times when their flame dwindles—and that's when we need each other the most.

At New Hope, we call these servants utility players. In baseball, a utility player can excel in several positions. These players can fill in wherever an unexpected need occurs. Utility players are worth their weight in gold!

Finding your place in ministry is wonderful, but being willing to serve wherever the need arises demonstrates the essence of a servant's heart.

A Sure Way to Win

I have found one sure way to win every baseball game, every basketball game and every football game. Would you like to know my secret? Here it is: Just have tons more players on your team than the other team fields.

"But that's against the rules!" you say.

Not in doing church as a team, it isn't. In fact, those *are* the rules! And you won't win without following them as passionately as you can manage.

"If the people don't want to come out to the ballpark," Yogi Berra once famously said, "nobody's going to stop them." With all due respect to Yogi, if you're committed to doing church as a team, it's your *job* not only to get them to the ballpark, but out of the stands and onto the playing field. Learn how to turn those spectators into players! And get them playing for the benefit of the church and the glory of God.

Team Preparation

1. List three of the greatest fears people have about getting involved in ministry.
   a.
   b.
   c.
2. What remedies can you give that could dispel each of these fears?
   a.
   b.
   c.
3. God is usually less interested in what you are doing than in what you are becoming. Make a list of some godly character qualities you have learned along the way. What specific circumstances helped you to develop these qualities?
4. List and discuss some of the fears people have when trying to include others in ministry.

C h a p t e r   9

SETTING YOUR COMPASS

Teach me Thy way, O LORD, and lead me in a level path.

PSALM 27:11

In Lewis Carroll's classic tale *Alice's Adventures in Wonderland*, young Alice encounters the Cheshire Cat during a hurried attempt to find her way through the maze of a fairy-tale forest.

"Would you tell me, please, which way I ought to go from here?" Alice cries.

"That depends a good deal on where you want to get to," the grinning Cat answers.

"I don't much care where—" a lost and flustered Alice says.

"Then it doesn't matter which way you go," says the Cat, who soon vanishes—all except for its toothy grin.[1]

Many people, ministries, and churches today feel as though they are staring at an enemy invisible except for a certain

Cheshire Cat grin. They've lost their sense of direction, so in the midst of their confused scampering, they look to different resources—conferences, audiotape series, the newest leadership book—to find answers. And although these may help for a season, they still have a nagging sense that something isn't quite right, that they're still missing the target.

(It's always easier to *imitate* than it is to *incarnate*, especially during a dry season when, as in 1 Samuel 3:1, a word from the Lord is rare and visions are infrequent.)

Exhausted from trying to implement the techniques that have worked for "successful" churches, they feel defeated. Oh, their hearts are right. In fact, their hearts are desperately seeking after God's best. And like Alice in Wonderland, they cry out, "Which way do I go?"

Starting at the Right Place

To reach a desired goal, you have to start at the right place and know where you're going.

Before you build a house, you need a blueprint. Before a plane leaves the tarmac, the pilot must file his flight plan. Before you do church as a team, you must have a clear and concise understanding of the mission and assignment the Lord has given specifically to your local church—what I refer to as *setting your compass* and what is commonly called *vision*.

Your vision is the goal God has set for your life and for your ministry. A clear vision provides the direction you seek for your ministry and your church. With a vision set firmly in place, you avoid scampering and confusion. Your compass is set, and you can be sure of your every step.

Each church has its own community, purpose, culture, passion and gifts. Because of the unique blend of all of these components, your church will have a unique vision. The first step—catching the vision—is absolutely critical, especially for pastors. There are no shortcuts.

God has a special, tailor-made vision for your church, just as He has one tailor-made for you, personally. This vision will become the very foundation of your ministry, the direction for your planning and the reason for your existence. By keeping this vision clearly fixed, you will have a much better chance of fulfilling His purposes. This is one of the most important aspects of doing church as a team: setting your compass through vision.

What Is a Vision?

A sculptor named Gutzon Borglum created a magnificent bust carving of Abraham Lincoln, now on view in the U.S. Capitol building under the Rotunda.

The story goes that a cleaning lady swept up for Borglum every day after he worked on sculpture. After many months the moment of the unveiling finally arrived. Gutzon Borglum invited his faithful cleaning lady to the inaugural showing as his personal guest.

As the velvet drape was drawn back, the room erupted with the sounds of awestruck admirers. The beauty of this work stunned the crowd. Smooth lines, the clear features of Lincoln's face, the jutting jaw and pronounced cheekbones, all expressed the touch of a master artist. The evening came to a close with the artist and the cleaning woman gazing at the finished piece of art that would adorn the Capitol for generations to come.

"Well, what do you think?" the sculptor asked.

After a brief moment, the faithful worker calmly replied, "I have only one question. How did you know that Mr. Lincoln was in that rock?"

Vision is the ability to see what others may not. It is the capacity to see potential—what things could be. Vision is the ability to see what God sees and the God-given motivation to bring to pass what you see. Whether it is a personal vision or a vision for a church, vision stirs up faith. You can't have one without the other. Faith will birth vision, and vision will fuel your faith.

Hebrews 11:1 describes this kind of vision: "Faith is the assurance of things hoped for, the conviction of things not seen." Faith is required to see the unseen, and by seeing what God has in store for your future, you begin to have vision. This means seeing not only with your eyes, but also with your heart.

But it is more than just having, as some define it, a "Big, Hairy, Audacious Goal" in mind. Vision may be a good exercise for getting your creative machinery rolling, but it is much more than that. It begins with the leaders toiling over and agreeing upon what God will hold you accountable for as a church on that Day. Of all the things we *can* do, what is it that we *must* do?

I suggest that you answer the following questions:

- Why did God place this ministry in this community?
- If this church could accomplish only four things, what would they be?
- How much of our ministry is geared toward the harvest, and how much is designed to take care of the grain?
- If our church had only a ten-year run and then shut down, what would its greatest priorities be?
- If I had only ten years left, what place would I take in all of this?
- What kind of potential lies within me that hasn't yet been tapped for the kingdom of God?

When you can conceive a clear, compelling picture of God's blueprint for your life or for the life of your church, you have vision! The clearer and the more compelling the picture, the more likely it is that others will catch the same vision. When everyone catches the vision, it becomes more than a vision; it is on its way to becoming a reality.

What is it that you can believe God wants to do through you? Much of your future will depend on your answer. Jesus Himself illustrated the importance of a person's answer:

> As Jesus left the house, he was followed by two blind men crying out, "Mercy, Son of David! Mercy on us!" When Jesus got home, the blind men went in with him. Jesus said to them, "Do you really believe I can do this?" They said, "Why, yes, Master!" He touched their eyes and said, *"Become what you believe."* It happened. They saw (Matt. 9:27-30, *THE MESSAGE*, emphasis added).

We become what we believe. If you can't believe that God will do something wonderful in your life, then you will have what you believe. But if you can believe, what awesome miracles will come to pass before your eyes!

I play the guitar. Not well, mind you, but I love the *sound* of the guitar. I have loved it for years. One day when I was living in Eugene, Oregon, my guitar teacher invited me to listen to a great jazz guitarist. This man produced the most beautiful, melodic lines I had ever heard. I sat in awe of how his skilled fingers moved with such ease and clarity. I turned to my teacher and said, "Man, I could never play like that!"

He turned to me and, as if to add emphasis to his words, slowly replied, "That's why you don't. You can't believe that you could do it. And you won't until you can *change your mind!*"

One man says, "I can." Another says, "I can't."

Which man is correct?

Both.

Scripture says, "For as [a man] thinks in his heart, so is he" (Prov. 23:7 *NKJV*). It's as simple as that. Whatever we envision for ourselves becomes what we eventually see in our lives.

Great vision, therefore, calls for the ability to see as God sees. It requires faith, but that's only one important element of vision, for vision begins in the seedbed of dreams.

It's Never Too Late to Start Dreaming

Dream lofty dreams, and as you dream, so shall you become.
Your vision is the promise of what you shall one day be!
JAMES ALLEN

The first step in finding your vision is to dream. God loves dreamers. Dreamers bring about the changes our world so desperately needs. God uses dreamers to turn dying churches into vibrant communities of excited, effective people.

God taught Abraham how to dream. He took Abraham outside of his tent and said, "Now look toward the heavens, and count the stars, if you are able to count them. . . . So shall your descendants be." When Abraham caught the vision and believed, God commended him and "reckoned it to him as righteousness" (Gen. 15:5-6). God wanted Abraham to have a clear picture of the end result of His promise. If Abraham should catch that vision, he would be able to see it come to pass in this world.

God's heart never changes. He still wants His children to catch clear pictures of the end results of His promises. He understands that in order for us to *be* it, we have to *see* it. And by faith, we catch sight of God's foresight.

In Joel 2:28, God lets us in on one aspect of the Holy Spirit's ministry to us in the last days:

> And it will come about after this that I will pour out My Spirit on all mankind; and your sons and daughters will prophesy, your old men will dream dreams, your young men will see visions.

Zero in with me on the phrase, "your old men will dream dreams." Let me suggest just one application for this promise: *It's never too late to start dreaming again!*

Many in the church have stopped dreaming, and without dreamers there can be no visionaries. Nothing changes until someone starts to dream. Maybe you think it's too late for you, that you'll never amount to anything. I have good news for you. One reason why the Holy Spirit is being poured out on us as Christians in these days is *so we can dream again!*

A church will never outgrow its vision, and no vision will ever exceed the church leaders' ability to dream. So dream big dreams for God! Some of us have lost motivation because we have stopped dreaming about the wonderful things God can do for our churches, our families and our future.

When Disney World in Orlando opened some years ago, the widow of the great entrepreneur stood with one of the engineers of the expansive new entertainment complex, gazing at its magnificence and beauty. The engineer, in a genuine effort to honor one of our country's greatest innovators, turned toward Mrs. Disney and remarked, "Boy, I wish Walt could have seen this!" Without taking her eyes off the sprawling play land, she replied, "He did. That's why it's here."

God wants us to start dreaming again. That's the beginning

of God-glorifying vision. Dream up the best you can for your life. If you are a pastor, dream up the best vision you can for the church. Fast-forward the tape of your mind 10 years down the road. If you had no restrictions whatsoever, what could you see for your church? Make the dream as lofty as you can. Even if it seems outrageous, fix it in your mind.

Got it?

Now read this verse from *The Living Bible*:

Now glory be to God who by his mighty power at work within us is able to do far more than we would ever dare to ask or even dream of—infinitely beyond our highest prayers, desires, thoughts, or hopes (Eph. 3:20).

Do you see what the Lord is saying? Go ahead, dream the biggest dreams you can, because as big as you can dream, God's dreams for you will always be bigger!

Begin with What You Have

At the beginning stages, you may tend to feel inadequate for the tasks ahead. You may feel ill-equipped to measure up to any new vision, let alone a God-glorifying dream. Rest assured, God will always start with what you have, not with what you don't have.

We can learn a lot about developing, or casting, vision by examining how God communicated vision to His people through His servant Moses.

Moses had the incredible assignment of guiding God's people out of Egypt, through the wilderness and into the Promised Land. Got vision? Moses sure did! The survival of God's people depended on nothing less than his ability to discern and then communicate this vision.

His powerful legacy set into motion vision and direction for every future generation of God's children. And among the greatest lessons the Lord gave Moses in communicating His vision was this: *begin with what you have.*

"The Lord spoke further to Moses, saying, 'Make yourself two trumpets of silver, of hammered work you shall make them; and you shall use them for summoning the congregation and for having the camps set out'" (Num. 10:1-2).

God told Moses to make these trumpets of silver—but where would recently freed slaves get their hands on precious metals? No jewelry stores dotted the neighborhood; no silver mines stood in their path. Fortunately, God had commanded the Israelites to plunder the wealth of the Egyptians prior to their departure, and so they had collected many articles of gold and silver (see Exod. 12:35-36). All of what God required, they already had within their grasp! The trumpets were to be made out of what they had, not from what they didn't possess.

As you begin to develop your vision, look at what you have. Look at the skills and talents, the spiritual gifts and passions God has planted in you. If you're developing a vision for your church, what precious commodities can be found within your people? God always starts with what you have. You never need to worry about implementing a vision beyond your grasp.

We remember David Livingstone as one of Christendom's greatest missionaries to Africa. Not only did he bring the gospel to the natives of this vast continent, but he also lived it—something that gave him great favor in the hearts of the people. After God called him to go deeper into the jungle to take the message of Jesus Christ to those who had never heard it, Livingstone encountered a remote tribe of the Congo. He learned that according to custom, he was to call for an audience with the tribal chief before entering the village. Failure to comply with this custom could have cost him his life.

Livingstone had to wait outside the village, with all his possessions lined up next to him. The chief, as a sign of acceptance, would take whatever he desired from among the missionary's possessions. To complete the exchange, the chief would give the guest something of his own. Then and only then would Livingstone be authorized to enter and share the gospel.

The scene resembled an orderly garage sale. Livingstone had set out his Bible, writing pad, clothes, shoes, blanket—and his goat. Livingstone suffered from a weak stomach that required him to drink goat's milk. The local drinking water was often questionable, so this was his answer to survival. Often Livingstone had asked God to heal his infirmity, but it seemed his lot to drink goat's milk every morning.

After what seemed an eternity to Livingstone, the chief emerged from his tent and made his way slowly toward the man of God about whom he had heard so much. Ornately attired in ivory and gold, the chief was followed closely by his advisers and priests. He surveyed the possessions of the missionary, while Livingstone silently prayed, *Lord, let him take anything he wants except my goat! You know I need its milk for my very survival. Lord, blind his eyes to the goat!*

The chief promptly walked over to the goat and pointed at it, and one of his advisors whisked the animal away. Livingstone stood stunned, as if his life had abruptly come to a halt.

A few moments later, the man who took his goat returned. In exchange, he handed Livingstone a stick, and left.

"A stick?!" the man of God cried. "Ridiculous! Here he takes my life's sustenance, and in return I get an old stick!"

A man standing close by, seeing Livingstone's confusion, quickly spoke. "Oh no! That is not a stick. My friend, that is the chief's very own scepter. With it, you will gain entry to every tribe and village in the interior. You have been given safe passage and great authority as a gift from the king!"

Then Livingstone realized what God had done. From that time forward, God's Word spread to uncounted thousands of native people. And, as a side note, Livingstone's stomach ailment was healed, too.

God never asks for more than we are able to handle, though times will come when it will be beyond what we are *able* to do. The difference is faith. God can bridge the difference; that's not the issue. The issue is what you have faith *for*. In the case of vision, be of great faith! Possess a confident assurance of the things you hope for, convinced beyond your comprehension and beyond circumstances that He is already working to fulfill them for you. Begin with what you have, faithful that God will fulfill the rest.

Blow a Clear Trumpet

Let's get back to Moses. Notice that God commanded Moses to "make yourself" these trumpets (Num. 10:1). Moses was not to buy them, rent them or borrow them from a local marching band. He was to hammer them out for himself and then learn to blow them until they sounded clearly. The trumpets would be used to call the congregation together, to summon the leaders, to warn the people and to bring organization to the nation's travel plans whenever God told them to move.

Once the Lord gives you a God-glorifying dream of what your ministry can be, the next step is to hammer it out. You'll catch a clear picture of His promise, but you must hammer out the details of how that dream will become reality—that's a critical step, probably the most time-consuming and the most important. This is where you begin laying out a clear path, or blueprint, for the future.

Hammering out the details requires the ability to see where a church is (point A) and where the church is going (point B), as well as how to take it from point A to point B. For example, let's say New Hope has a weekly attendance of about 10,000 members. This is our point A. Our vision may be that in three or four years, we should be at 15,000. That's point B. Next we need to hammer out a trumpet to produce that clear call.

In this case, we would need to have facilities that can hold and serve 15,000 people at a time. We'll also need to beef up our Front Lines ministry, which produces our weekend services, so that they continue to feel inviting and alive. For that to happen, we have to have good administration and strong internal communications; the leader with the vision must project a clear goal to the congregation; and so forth. We'll also need to establish a greater platform of volunteer leaders—one that grows proportionately with the size of the church. That way we don't burn anybody out.

Then we make sure that we have an effective discipleship program, so that when new people come to faith in Christ, they will immediately get nurtured in a discipleship group. That means we'll have to bolster our small-group ministry, since we're a church of small groups and that's how we meet the needs of the people. When everybody participates in a small group, we enjoy connectedness.

That's what it's going to take to make this goal become a reality. In order to some day have a functioning church of 15,000 members, we'll have to set up the infrastructure for it today.

When city planners first thought of building a freeway in Hawaii, nobody took the proposal seriously. They laughed. Most people could not see the need for a three-lane highway connecting the then-small town of Honolulu to the rest of the island. Hawaii had very few car owners, and most had little reason to leave their countryside homes and businesses to come into town. Today, Hawaii's population has rocketed to 1.5 million. More than half of those people live on the small island of Oahu and work in the sprawling city of Honolulu. Gridlock grinds our rush hours to a standstill, and everyone wonders why the planners didn't have a bigger vision to begin with.

You can't get along without foresight when producing a vision. Take the time to plot your course carefully in the beginning, so you won't have to make major course corrections in the future. The time you spend on this will save you many sorrows in the years to come. If you pastor a church, you'll need to hammer out a couple of silver trumpets, based on your gifts and leadership style. You may use the same materials, same purpose and same assignment that the church used before, but hammer them out again until they blow clearly for you!

Custom Trumpets Only, Please!

The harder the conflict, the more glorious the triumph. What we obtain too cheap, we esteem too lightly; 'tis dearness only that gives everything its value.
THOMAS PAINE, *THE AMERICAN CRISIS*

You can find trumpets for sale everywhere, trumpets forged and hammered out by others. They will be for sale and readily available in every city, at most conferences, through the magazines and by mail order—but don't buy them! You can get trumpets from Chicago, Los Angeles, Korea, Toronto, Brownsville or even Hawaii. But don't do it. Hammer yours out for yourself! Sure, it will take some time and effort, but it will be well worth it. Only then will the trumpets blow clearly.

So what should we take back from others' ministries?

Take back *hammering techniques.* Learn principles and new perspectives, but don't buy ready-made trumpets. The reason those trumpets work so well in their own communities is that the leaders have taken the time to hammer them out for themselves. Each of us must do the same!

> *When you attend a conference, read a leadership book (even this one) or hear about the latest move of God in another church, do not superimpose that vision onto your own church.*

Only you can know the needs and discern the distinct call that God has for your life, for your ministry and, if you're a pastor, for your church. No one else will know your ministry the way you do. And when you take the time to hammer it out, you will find a depth of understanding and a quality that could never be attained any other way. You'll begin to blow a clarion sound that will help others to catch the vision to do church as a team.

We have felt privileged to partner with Willow Creek Community Church of South Barrington, Illinois. By partnering, I mean that we attended many of their conferences and took copious notes on how they became one of the most successful churches in America.

Now, although we have the highest esteem for the folks at Willow Creek, we would never dream of creating a cookie-cutter copy of their Chicago-area church in Hawaii. It would never work. Why not? Because we have two very different constituencies—two very distinct congregations. We did, however, apply some of their hammering techniques in the way we pounded out our own trumpet. Whereas Willow Creek has a food court filled with Midwest cuisine, like hot dogs, we have potlucks laden with the many ethnic dishes of Hawaii. We enjoyed their website design and adapted our own site to reflect a similar innovative "realness" to appeal to the people of Hawaii.

When you attend a conference, read a leadership book (even this one) or hear about the latest move of God in another church, do not superimpose that vision onto your own church. Learn all you can, of course, for a desire to continually learn is the mark of a visionary. But remember that simplistic duplication has no value, and in fact, may hurt your organization.

Learn hammering techniques; don't copy styles. Learn how they do what they do well, but don't buy their trumpet and attempt to play the same tune back home. Your people will have a unique style, as unique as the flavor of their foods and the sound of their music. Honor your people by hammering out your own trumpet for your own church.

Two Trumpets Are Eternally Better Than One

> And when both are blown, all the congregation shall gather themselves to you at the doorway of the tent of meeting. Yet if only one is blown, then the leaders, the heads of the divisions of Israel, shall assemble before you. But when you blow an alarm, the camps that are pitched on the east side shall set out (Num. 10:3-5).

This Scripture reveals a couple of other interesting vision-building principles. First, God designated different trumpet blasts for different purposes. Second, Moses was to make for himself *two* trumpets. God designed it this way so that Moses had to recruit and train others from the very beginning. Moses had only one set of lips, of course, so someone had to shadow Moses and learn what he knew. God wanted them to lead as a team!

Our success as servant-leaders will depend in large part on bringing others alongside us who know the vision, live the vision and help cast the vision. Moses didn't have forever on this side of eternity. He had to have a replacement, and God made provision for Israel's future leaders at the inception of the process.

Even in our own lives and ministries, there's just too much to do for one person to do it all alone. Bring other servant-leaders alongside you, share the wealth of ministry that's available, and never, ever go it alone. That's a surefire prescription for ministry suicide.

Next, we must begin writing out our vision. Consider several guidelines to help you become the wordsmith of a great vision.

Guidelines for a God-Glorifying Vision

Every church needs a clear vision with certain qualities to ensure that the vision indeed glorifies God:

1. *The vision must be birthed and aligned with the Word of God.* God's Word is infallible; our desires or goals are not. Be sure that the Bible confirms your dreams and that it never conflicts with them. Does a key verse or passage embody your vision? Ask God to reveal it to you; He will. "All Scripture is inspired by God and profitable for teaching, for reproof, for correction,

for training in righteousness; that the man of God may be adequate, equipped for every good work" (2 Tim. 3:16-17).

2. *The vision must be consistent with the Great Commission for reaching the lost.* Every church should have at its core a passion for the lost. We can have goals for success, nurturing and discipleship, but if we are not bringing people to Christ, we have missed the point. "Go therefore and make disciples of all the nations, baptizing them in the name of the Father and the Son and the Holy Spirit, teaching them to observe all that I commanded you" (Matt. 28:19-20).

3. *The vision must be hammered out.* Your whole heart must be in the vision, and this is best accomplished by hammering out your own trumpet/vision for your life and your ministry. If your heart is not in it—if it is simply another program from another ministry—you will not pursue it aggressively. If God has indeed given you a vision, then He will give you the passion to fuel that vision and see it come to pass. He will also make available all the resources needed to see it through. "Make two silver trumpets for yourself; you shall make them of hammered work" (Num. 10:2).

4. *The vision must be clear, concise and easily understood by everyone.* Make sure the language you use to communicate the vision is clear, easily understood and to the point. If all are to catch the vision, they must first understand what it means, and everyone must catch the vision to guarantee complete success. "Then the Lord answered me and said, 'Record the vision and inscribe it on tablets, that the one who reads it may run'" (Hab. 2:2).

5. *The vision must guide every activity.* Vision cannot be a neat platitude or a nice saying in a booklet somewhere. It must be the compass that guides all your activities. Churches without a clear commission or statement of purpose are like ships without rudders. Make the vision plain and always visible as a reminder of God's call for the church. "If you know these things, you are blessed if you do them" (John 13:17).

The writer of Hebrews admonishes us to "run with endurance the race that is set before us" (Heb. 12:1). Each of us is accountable to run the race that God has set before us. Every church has a specific, unique assignment and direction, and we will stand accountable before God for the completion and fulfillment of that call. No two churches are the same. Each has its own unique style, or thumbprint, and its vision must be processed and refined until everyone feels an ownership in it.

Remember this: People need a vision, but a vision also needs people! You can have a vision, but if nobody buys into it, you don't have anything.

We must all have the commitment to jump into the things of the kingdom of God with reckless abandon and "get wild" for Him. We must have the passion to do whatever it takes. We must be like the disciples of Jesus and say, "We're gonna go for it! We've got one chance to serve Jesus before He comes, when we will go to heaven forever and never see a non-Christian for all of eternity. This is our only chance to do something to make a difference." When you catch that fire in your bosom, *then* things start to happen. When you catch a glimpse of eternity, you'll feel the flames of urgency licking at your heart and firing your vision, and you will truly understand that vision is vital to the survival of your church and your ministry.

How New Hope Did It

With the fire of a clear vision burning in our hearts, and with these principles and guidelines set in place, New Hope ventured into the process of developing our own vision. We understood the tremendous importance of a clear and compelling vision, but pounding out our vision was by no means an easy task. Nevertheless, it was well worth the time, heart and effort we poured into this foundation of our church.

We started with the first two steps, aligning our vision with the Word of God, especially the Great Commission:

> Go therefore and make disciples of all the nations, baptizing them in the name of the Father and the Son and the Holy Spirit, teaching them to observe all that I commanded you; and lo, I am with you always, even to the end of the age (Matt. 28:19-20).

This is the heart of Jesus for the church as well as for the lost. These were His final words on Earth, a charge to venture into the world. This one statement gives us the starting point for all our assignments, and it is here that we at New Hope found our call.

We noticed that the Great Commission can be broken into four distinct stages. Each of these stages comprises one of New Hope's four "pillars" that support our church and make up our major ministry clusters.

Stage One: EVANGELISM

The first word of Matthew 28:19 tells us to "go." Jesus calls us to take the initiative and reach out. This means action! We call this stage *evangelism*. This is simply leading non-Christians to the

Lord so that they become transformed, forgiven, growing followers of Christ.

We designed our Sunday morning services to partner with our members in their attempts to win their friends and families to Christ. The ambiance, printed materials, music and message are all shaped to support this goal.

One of our mottos at New Hope says that we connect everything to a soul. Whether it's a video, a song, printed material or an activity, we always ask ourselves: "Could we invite a non-Christian to this?"

We must always keep our hearts toward the harvest. As I've said before, the harvest will not self-reap, but it will self-destruct if not reaped. So at New Hope, we connect everything we do to a soul. It is not a program. Evangelism is not a class we take but a culture we have developed. It is the air we breathe, the atmosphere, the very mentality of New Hope.

Stage Two: EDIFICATION

The second stage is discipleship: "Make disciples of all the nations." We call this stage *edification*, which means building up each individual in his or her faith. God never said to fill the churches with converts; He said to fill them with disciples.

Our goal at New Hope is to take a convert and build him or her into a disciple of the Lord. This is where our small groups and midweek services come in. We have a course and tape series called *Growing Deep, Growing Strong* that introduces each person to membership.

A critical aspect of this stage is getting each new convert into a self-feeding program. We emphasize the priority of doing daily devotions and how to sit at Jesus' feet and learn from Him.

The Life Journal is one of the most important aspects of this stage. Literally thousands of those who make New Hope their home church are involved in Life Groups in which members regularly read the Bible together in a systematic way as a family of believers. This has formed the foundation of everything we do.

You can find out more about Life Groups from our website, www.enewhope.org, where you can order journals. No other program has done as much for us as this one has. This, bar none, is the most critical aspect of the EDIFICATION stage.

Stage Three: EQUIPPING

The third stage points to a further *equipping*, in which God encourages each of us to "observe all I have commanded you." Herein lies the beginning of fruitfulness and life transformation. This means putting into practice what we understand. It is not just in the knowing but in doing that we are blessed. Jesus tells us, "If you know these things, *you are blessed if you do them*" (John 13:17, emphasis added).

The New Hope DESIGN course and Doing Church as a Team conferences play a large part in this stage. We equip people when we help them discover, develop and deploy their gifts. Each person is encouraged to put his or her gifts into action so that God's promise for their lives can be fulfilled, even as they realize the fullness of their faith.

Our EQUIPPING stage is designed to get people "out of the pews" and "onto the playing field." We began a Bible college to further the equipping of young leaders. Along with that, our intern program allows leaders to train with New Hope. It turns knowing into doing, receiving into giving—and so we squeeze the sponge!

Stage Four: EXTENSION

Finally, Jesus calls us to courageously reach out to others. The Lord assures us that He will accompany us: "And lo, I am with you, even until the end of the age." We call this stage *extension*, in which we close the loop, with all of us reaching out and inviting someone else, even as we were invited.

God never told the world to come to the church; He told the church to "go into all the world" (Mark 16:15). Therefore, each of us must take the initiative to reach out to our families and friends, inviting them to Jesus. And each church must take the initiative to take Jesus to the people.

Through EXTENSION we reach into the community with practical, seed-planting efforts. We put gloves on the gospel. We take the ways of God and communicate them in ways that non-believers can understand.

For many in our communities, the church down the street seems disconnected with the reality of life. The congregation arrives on Sundays and disappears almost as quickly as it showed up. They watch this happen year after year, and except for a few feeble attempts to recruit new people, only rarely does the church engage with the community.

We have a way to check ourselves to see how our credibility fares with the members of our community. If a non-Christian in our immediate community were to tell us why they like New Hope, what would she or he say?

"I like New Hope in our community because they _____." (You fill in the blank.)

The reason can't be "because they own property," or "they hold services."

WHY would people feel excited that you are in their

community? Wouldn't it be wonderful to hear them say something like one of the following:

- "Because they tutored my kids"
- "Because they have an after school sports program"
- "Because they cleaned our park"
- "Because they counseled my son who was on drugs"
- "Because they painted the local school gym that had run down"
- "Because they hold an exercise class for seniors"

Any of these answers will help make the gospel credible to those who live in your community. A few years ago, we saw many young children entering school from a lower income area. We decided that we could express our love by giving all the incoming first graders a bag of school supplies, including pencils, crayons, a notebook, a ruler, paste and a few other items that all young students need. When parents saw this, for the first time they saw our church as *helpful* to them and a *credible part* of their community.

Interestingly, the four stages—evangelism, edification, equipping and extension—build on one another. *They flow naturally, marking each phase of the maturing process of every Christian— from salvation to disciple to fruitful leader who will then go out and reach others for Christ.* This is the beauty of God's master plan.

From these four stages, inspired by the Great Commission, came the mission statement of New Hope Christian Fellowship:

The purpose of New Hope is to present the gospel of Jesus Christ in such a way that turns non-Christians into converts (EVANGELISM), converts into disciples (EDIFICATION) and disciples into mature, fruitful leaders

(EQUIPPING), who will in turn go into the world and reach others for Christ (EXTENSION).

This mission guides everything we do. It is the trumpet of New Hope that we use to summon our people to God's purposes. It must be blown consistently and clearly in order for us to paddle together as a team, each of us heading in the same direction with the same heart and the same goals.

Your church must find its own course, its own race and its own calling. Only then will you be able to confidently set your compasses and navigate the ocean of decisions ahead of you.

In science as in the church, if a basic premise is incorrect, all subsequent conclusions will be in error. If we feel unsure of our premise, our purpose or our values, then every conclusion we draw will come up short. Our confidence in our calling will feel shaky, at best. A sure foundation comes from a compelling vision, and that starts with a God-given dream.

A Powerful Dream

I see a powerful dream springing up in the hearts of God's churches today, a dream with an edge to it, a vision. And that vision is becoming a rallying banner uniting the hearts of God's people.

This dream is nothing new. It's as old as the Bible itself. In fact, you'll find this dream within the excellent pages of the Word, which commands us to go forth and make disciples of all the nations as one Body—the Body of Christ.

We are many churches uniquely commissioned, but in Christ unified. Through our common identity as the Body of Christ, we express to our world the fullness of who Jesus is. That's what the church is designed to do. That's His great plan for all of us. That's how we become the fulfillment of God's great plan, for together we can obey God more fully than any one of us could alone.

Team Preparation

1. What is your church's mission statement? Can you write it from memory? Where is this mission statement displayed?

2. If you've been to a conference lately, what hammering techniques have you learned? Why are these better than buying ready-made trumpets?

3. If you are a ministry leader in your church, write a mission statement for your ministry, making sure that it is in line with your church's overarching mission statement.

4. What is *your* dream? What God-given, God-designed dream has He planted in your heart? If you had no obstacles whatsoever, what would you do? Why aren't you doing that now? How can you begin to move in that direction?

5. If you strongly disagree with and cannot subscribe to your church's mission statement, what should you do?

Note

1. Lewis Carroll, *Alice's Adventures in Wonderland*, in Martin Gardner, *The Annotated Alice* (New York: New American Library, 1960), p. 88.

C h a p t e r   1 0

ALIGNMENT: THE POWER OF MOVING TOGETHER

Then the LORD answered me and said, "Record the vision and inscribe
it on tablets, that the one who reads it may run."

HABAKKUK 2:2

When I pastored a church in the small town of Hilo on the Big
Island of Hawaii, my wife, Anna, and I decided to become an
official American family and purchase a minivan. We went
shopping and picked out the perfect one (the model my love-
ly wife liked). We proudly drove home in our new minivan,

and all was well—or so we thought.

Within a few weeks, my wife began to notice a problem with the handling of our new vehicle. She astutely diagnosed the trouble with the words, "It's driving a little funny." So I hopped in to give it a whirl, certain that the problem couldn't be anything major. Sure enough, the minivan stubbornly veered to one side of the road; I had to strain at the wheel to steer it back to center. Any way I turned, the vehicle pulled strongly to the right—so much so that I had to drive crooked to go straight!

So I took the car to a mechanic friend of mine. When he asked what seemed to be the problem, I sheepishly echoed my wife: "It's driving a little funny."

He nodded understandingly, the wise sage of all things mechanical and technical. He looked under the hood and then hoisted the minivan on a lift to inspect the underside. Finally he said, "It's your alignment. It's off. That's why the whole car pulls to one side when it should be going forward."

This master of the monkey wrench taught me a lesson in alignment. He told me that *any vehicle out of alignment cannot function to its potential.* The wheels won't run straight unless they remain aligned. Sure, you can still go forward in either case—but when things are aligned, they go forward with much less wear.

Consider the locust. Scripture says, "The locusts have no king, yet all of them go out in ranks" (Prov. 30:27). Despite their diminutive size and their status as pests, the locusts receive honorable mention in the Word of God. What is it about these small insects that merits such an honor?

Have you ever seen a swarm of locusts? The swarm moves in uncanny ways. It appears as a dark, writhing cloud, moving steadily and posing a serious threat to every blade of grass and patch of green in its path. Even given the advantages of modern technology, farmers remain largely helpless to prevent locusts from devastating their crops. Locusts are among the smallest of creatures, but they become a mighty force when they move *en masse.*

That's the power of moving together—the power of alignment.

Defining Alignment

The strength of any vision lies in alignment—that is, *vision caught and shared by every person involved.* A common vision is the product of every person living a life of character and hearing the same call, a shared picture of a preferred, God-designed future. If you want to build a strong team, you have to get everyone pulling together for the same cause.

Vision means little without alignment. You can have the most visionary ideals, but without alignment, you will be unable to achieve them. Without everyone in your church catching a common vision, success will remain beyond your reach. You need a common vision in order to arrive at a common goal.

If there's one thing worse than a church without vision, it's a church with many visions. In such a congregation, everyone lobbies for his or her own personal agenda, and the church ends up becoming a political assembly—not a single body, but a chaotic gathering of conflicted individuals, each one pulling for his or her own viewpoint. With too many visions, a church sows the seeds of dissension at its very inception and ensures its own failure. An old Greek proverb says, If you pursue two hares, both will escape you.

What happens when people lack a common vision? Simply this: Even though you are together, you have no idea where you are going. Always remember, people without a vision perish (see Prov. 29:18, *KJV*). No amount of congregational unity will compensate for a lack of pastoral vision. Without a clear and compelling vision, all will fail and the ministry will go to waste. Such a ministry will bear little fruit, because the people won't know where God is leading them. They won't know what purpose they are meant to fulfill. "For if the bugle produces an indistinct sound, who will prepare himself for battle?" (1 Cor. 14:8). Without alignment, disharmony and disunity will prevail.

The apostle Paul wrote to the church at Philippi, "Make my joy complete by being of the same mind, maintaining the same love, united in spirit, intent on one purpose" (Phil. 2:2). Here Paul speaks about the joy of everyone in a group possessing the same heart and passion. He knew of nothing more beautiful than a congregation in which everyone marches from the same starting point, with the same heart, in the same direction and with the same cadence. This produces a joyous song with great rhythm and beautiful harmony.

Alignment can help build an unstoppable movement with the power to overcome every obstacle, move every mountain and bridge every impasse. With everyone in alignment, every activity contributes in a more meaningful way to the overall vision of the church.

Recording the Vision

To build alignment, you must first let the people know where they are supposed to be headed. *Alignment begins when every member understands your direction and echoes it in his or her heart.*

My responsibility as a servant-leader is to shepherd God's people by setting forth a mission statement, or statement of purpose, for the people He asks me to lead. I must communicate the vision if the people are to catch it.

Each person has been called to run the race to win (see Heb. 12:1-2), but it is the leader's call to set the vision clearly before the people so that they may run well. In his short but powerful Old Testament book, the prophet Habakkuk gives us this vital principle for building alignment:

> Then the LORD answered me and said, "Record the vision and inscribe it on tablets, *that the one who reads it may run.* For the vision is yet for the appointed time; it hastens toward the goal, and it will not fail. Though it tarries, wait for it; for it will certainly come, it will not delay" (Hab. 2:2-3, emphasis added).

God tells leaders to set a statement of purpose clearly before the people so that they may run in such a way that they will win. Knowing the vision and presenting it clearly are crucial to the success of any church or ministry.

At New Hope Christian Fellowship, we continually communicate our mission statement and core values to the whole church. We explain our vision and disseminate it in as many ways as we can—from the pulpit, in our newsletters, in weekly bulletins and in most of our flyers. We even post it in the reception area of our offices so that anyone who walks in, whether visitor or member, can read it and know what we're doing. When we can all see the vision (the assignment of our church), we can all run together.

Even though we may have heard it many times before, we remind ourselves of the common vision so that we stay in tune with each other and with our original purpose. That's a lesson we can take from the locusts. Though they have no king, they go out in ranks because they remain single-minded in their purpose. Although we *do* have a King, we must be sure to check in regularly to know fully His mission for us, so that we can go out in ranks with a common call on our hearts.

God has called us to be a people of vision, with every one of us pulling together in rhythm. Since everyone has a paddle, everyone has a part. In order for our canoe to arrive successfully at its destination, the people need to row together. We all must stroke together and not stroke at our own pace. Paddling together propels us forward and results in progress.

New churches often split after a year or two because their leaders don't understand these principles. God placed these principles in the Scriptures so that every leader can tuck them deep within his or her heart. If you are a leader, set these principles firmly in your heart.

Take God's vision and write it down clearly, then teach your people to have a common vision. If they can't submit to that vision, then it's not the place or ministry where God wants them. You *must* have unity among the brethren. When you have unity within your ministry, your people will go forth together. And like the locusts, who have no king but go out in ranks, the people who have caught the vision of your ministry will not need a leader constantly supervising them. You can release them to run!

Arrows Pointing in the Same Direction

What does alignment look like? If we were to draw a picture of alignment, it should not look like a cloud (though that seems to work for locusts). Instead, let's represent each member or ministry of the congregation as an arrow to show that each of us has his or her own direction.

If we all agree with the overall mission of the church, then all of our arrows point in the same direction. When we're not in alignment, we look like a mess of pick-up sticks scattered on the ground.

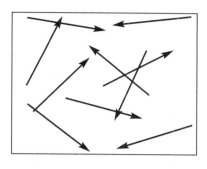 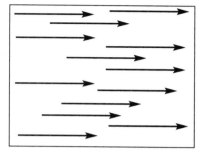

Church Without Alignment   *Church with Alignment*

Which of these represents the flow of your ministry?

Whatever your situation, it's never too late to make adjustments and repair your alignment. The fact is, even if we are generally in alignment, we can stay in alignment only if we frequently make midcourse corrections—adjustments to the way we do church. We all have a natural tendency to shift during transit, like automobile wheels reacting to bumps and curves in the road. So we must make constant minor course corrections, just as we do when we drive our cars, or else we risk straying from the road and missing our goal.

Constantly Evaluating for Success

Just as our bodies have many internal organs, so our churches will have many ministries—ministries for youth, men, women, small groups and children, to name a few. When in proper alignment, these ministries directly fulfill the church's overarching vision. They constantly check to make sure their arrows (their hearts and direction of their ministry) point in the same direction as the mission of the church. To do that, each ministry must continually review its strategy for fulfilling that general vision.

Each ministry must constantly evaluate itself, asking the following questions:

- Is our ministry producing disciples and mature leaders integrated into the context of the church? Or is the ministry an island unto itself with independent goals?
- In what way do we share vision with volunteers and staff? Is this method effective?
- How is my relationship with those who supervise me? Are we friends or just related by ministry?
- How do we regain alignment? Do we need to make any course corrections within our ministry or church?

When each ministry and every member pulls together in the same direction, then you begin doing church as a team. Synergy in this combined effort far exceeds the strength of a single person or small group of individuals trying to do it alone. In fact, two people doing the same task together will produce much more than twice the effort of a single person—and three or more people doing church together increases synergy exponentially.

Not only do physical energy and wisdom double when we do church as a team, but we also gain anointing. Jesus promised, "Where two or three have gathered together in My name, there I am in their midst" (Matt. 18:20).

Make sure to keep that synergy and anointing by constantly reevaluating yourself, your ministry and your church. Ask yourself those key questions and take care that you're still on track. If you're not, no problem. Make any necessary corrections—and no matter what, keep going!

Defining Values

In the first phase of successful alignment, you constantly evaluate your ministry. In the second phase, you have to identify your ministry's core values.

A church's core values gives each person a point of reference—a ministry North Star that provides your people with a sense of direction and cohesion.

Values are like windows through which decisions get viewed. When confronted with a certain choice, we will tend to make the choice most consistent with our values. Common values give

> *When people in the church make decisions consistent with the core values, you achieve a wonderful synergy and a culture of balance and truth.*

everyone the same starting point and the same perspective. When people in the church make decisions consistent with the core values, you achieve a wonderful synergy and a culture of balance and truth.

Values can also be likened to a homing device, an internal guidance mechanism that keeps you on course. Values help you to make in-flight corrections to your attitudes, motives, activities and emphases. Each of us needs to make many in-flight corrections along the way, but if we have not clearly defined our core values, we won't know when or how to make course corrections. When a church's values are understood and echoed in the heart of every member, you have alignment.

Some years ago, I took a week of golf lessons. My instructor wanted to teach me the feel of a basic swing and how the ball should fly if I hit it correctly. He geared the whole week toward that single goal. Without knowing how to correctly swing and what the flight of the ball should look like, I would have no point of reference for improving my swing. Even if I happened to hit a great shot, I wouldn't know what I had done to create it, and I wouldn't be able to repeat it if I tried. Conversely, should I hit a terrible shot, I would have no idea why it went bad or how to correct it.

That's just like the church sometimes, isn't it? We often just swing away, never knowing why sometimes we hit the mark and why at others we miss it so badly. We may chalk up the results to a divine blessing or a demonic attack, depending on the outcome, when really it has more to do with us not knowing our point of reference.

Knowing our core values is like knowing the basic golf swing—it sets a baseline that can guide us in knowing when we're hitting it and when we're missing it. That way we'll know which opportunities we get to say yes to and which ones we get to say no to. Commonly understood values help us to set our sights on the vision and increase our chances of achieving and maintaining alignment.

Wrestling with a Vision for Values

We are to catch our vision and values from the Lord and wrestle with them until we can articulate them clearly to others. This does not come easily.

Sometimes the Lord will reveal all in a moment, but not usually. Often we are like Jacob, who wrestled all night until he saw daylight (see Gen. 32:24). Most leaders find that they must wrestle with their vision until the values become clear. This process may feel both heart- and soul-wrenching, but again, there are no shortcuts.

At New Hope our declaration of nine core values grew out of a host of discussions about what we valued. I talked with dozens of leaders, received input from as many members as I could and tested the list over and over again by seeking further feedback, knowing that identifying these values would help us to clarify what is truly important and where we should focus our energies and resources.

Inspired by what I saw, I made a point to get alone and pray during this process. I went on a spiritual retreat to hear from the Lord about His will for our church. My retreats usually consist of getting away for two or three days to a neighboring island, where I isolate myself in a hotel to pray. During these times I am best able to hear direction for my life and for the church.

I also went on a retreat with our management team to help formulate the vision and shape the core values of the church.

This wrestling extracted the best from us: in-depth discussions followed, we prayed and fasted, and we sought the Lord's face for our church. But when we finished, the daylight streamed in and we had nine core values that provided the reference point for every activity, every service and every member of New Hope Community Church.

New Hope's Nine Core Values

At New Hope, our values function like a metronome that keeps us all paddling with the same cadence. We hold tightly to these nine core values. These principles flavor every activity and balance every endeavor. Each member wholeheartedly subscribes to each one. In doing so, we can all have "the same love, united in spirit, intent on one purpose" (Phil. 2:2).

1. We believe that every person, Christian and non-Christian alike, is valuable to God and to His kingdom.

Because people are eternally valuable to God, they are valuable to us as well. Responsible evangelism will always be our cause, and ongoing discipleship will always be the core of the ministry (see Matt. 18:14; Matt. 25:45; 2 Pet. 3:9).

People are precious. They rank very high on God's ledger, and if we are going to be a people after God's own heart, they had better rank pretty high on ours as well! We must love them with His love and care for them with His compassion. People are eternal, and their eternal welfare is much more important than their present behavior. Looking past who they are and seeing them for what they can be will always open new doorways to ministry and to unexpected miracles.

This doesn't mean we become people pleasers. We are here to please an audience of One! Loving people means that we remain committed to God's very best for their lives. If God's best means overlooking a fault or indiscretion, then we overlook it. If God's best is to confront, then we will confront in love.

Even in the case of evangelism, we must become sensitive to a person's readiness to receive the gospel. We Christians can be insensitive in our evangelism; in our zeal to convert unbelievers, we can do more damage than good. Responsible evangelism and ongoing discipleship are central to our calling.

2. We believe that doing church as a team is God's design for effective ministry.

Spirit-empowered service, with the willing-hearted involvement of every person, is vital to accomplishing God's plan (see Ps. 133:1; Eccles. 4:9-12; Eph. 4:11-16; 1 Pet. 2:4-9).

The day of the Lone Ranger is over. If we are going to be

effective in this new century, everyone in the church must realize his or her importance to God's plan. We are called the Body of Christ, not the collection of Christ's body parts. Everyone has a place, a function and a purpose; but we've got to learn to work together. There's just no substitute! And the more people who take ownership of the ministry, the stronger a church becomes.

3. We believe that a simple presentation of Jesus Christ in creative ways will impact and transform lives.
We will always keep the balance of relating to our culture through redeeming the arts, even while remaining true to the Scriptures. This allows us to present the gospel in such a way that it reaches the heart (see Acts 17:22-24; 1 Cor. 9:22-23).

People aren't tired of the gospel; they're tired of tired presentations of the gospel. The gospel is the power of God to transform lives! It isn't boring; it is powerful. When the gospel is preached, the Holy Spirit takes down-and-out drug addicts and turns them into saints. He takes broken marriages and restores them. He takes hopeless lives and breathes new beginnings into them. But remember this: The Holy Spirit's responsibility is to assure that the message is true, not necessarily interesting. That's *our* responsibility!

So while remaining true to the Scriptures, we work through creative ways to present the claims of Christ. We will use anything we can to help people understand just how wonderful and precious the Word of God is. Hebrews tells us that the Word is "living and active" (Heb. 4:12), so if we can plant it deep in a person's soul, the Lord will do the rest. But first, we must use good soil so that the seed can take root.

I remember when this fact first struck me. I was reading Matthew 13, the parable of the sower and the seed. Jesus describes the varying soils into which seed gets sown, and He likens them to the varying responses of the human heart. Only once does the devil enter the story. And how does the devil find entry?

> When anyone hears the word of the kingdom, *and does not understand it*, the evil one comes and snatches away what has been sown in his heart (Matt. 13:19, emphasis added).

When someone doesn't understand the Word sown in his or her heart, the devil takes the opportunity to snatch it away. That hit me like a ton of bricks! I thought, *If I am the preacher and I am sowing the Word, then I must do my best to make sure each listener understands. What they do with it after that is up to them, but I must communicate in such a way that the truth impacts their hearts. I've just got to be sure they understand it!*

For weeks and months I thought about this. I knew the good news needed to be made simple to understand, creative in presentation and accurate in content. I had to take the cookies off the top shelf and put them on the lower shelf, so everyone could grasp them. I just *had* to help people understand the gospel!

If multimedia helps, then I will use it. If a dance, a mime, a song or a sketch will better present the gospel so that people can better understand it, then I will redeem that method for the gospel's sake. If by tap dancing I could help people's eyes see the truths of the Bible, then I would learn to tap dance.

We will not use multimedia or the performing arts just because we want to be part of the latest trend or because other churches are doing so. We use the arts because we can help people to better understand the Word. We will never compromise the truths or accuracy of the Bible for the sake of an art form.

God's Word never changes, but cultures do. Therefore, we will anchor ourselves to His ageless truths, but gear the style through which we present those truths to the times we are living in.

4. We believe every member should commit to a lifestyle of consistent spiritual growth, with honest accountability.
A genuine love for God is always a first priority (see Mark 12:30). Every Christian should yearn for continual spiritual growth. Therefore, discipleship through small groups, accountability and open honesty are critical to maturing in our faith (see Prov. 27:17; Mark 12:31; Acts 2:44-47; 1 Tim. 4:7-8; 1 Pet. 2:2).

There are two kinds of Christians in the world today: One knows what to do, and the other does what he or she knows. Our ranks are crowded with the first—a serious problem. It's easy to recognize the symptoms. Many of us know all about joy but display none of it in our families. We know all about forgiveness but we just can't seem to forgive our spouses or parents.

Small groups provide one of the best ways to bridge this discrepancy. In these huddles of friends, we can support one another, graciously remind one another of what we believe, and hold each other accountable. Pretenses get minimized when you get up close and personal!

5. We believe that every member is a minister who has been given gifts to be discovered, developed and deployed.
We are a gift-based, volunteer-driven church. Each believer will find his greatest joy and fulfillment when serving in his gifts and passion. Every believer is created for ministry, gifted for ministry, authorized for ministry and needed for ministry (see Mark 10:45; Rom. 12; 1 Cor. 12:14-20; Eph. 2:10).

No one is unimportant! I continually remind our members that somewhere, in some context, everyone is a 10. God has deposited within each of us one or more gifts through which we can make an eternal contribution. As each person finds his or her place and begins serving through his or her gifts, the church will run together with maximum effectiveness and minimum weariness.

6. We believe that God is worthy of our very best. Therefore, a growing spirit of excellence should permeate every activity.
Not perfection, but excellence with consistent evaluation and a willingness to improve for the sake of the kingdom of God, mark growing ministries (see Ps. 78:72; Eccles. 10:10; Dan. 5:12; Col. 3:17).

There is no greater vision, no more compelling invitation, than to serve the King of kings! He is indeed worthy of our very best.

We serve an excellent God, and because we are created in His image, we can be an excellent people. Excellence can be truly achieved in our actions only when it first appears in the heart behind our actions.

7. We believe that genuine love and caring relationships are key to the life of every endeavor.
Refusing to give audience to a spirit of complaining, we will instead courageously solve every problem in a way that honors God and builds biblical character. We value healthy relationships and will protect the unity of the Spirit in our church (see Rom. 16:17; 1 Cor. 13:8; Eph. 4:3; Jas. 1:2-3; 1 Pet. 5:8-9).

One element common to all growing churches is problems.

They come with the territory. Growing pains—such as crowded parking lots, long lines and short-handed classrooms—will continue to plague expanding twenty-first-century ministries. We have decided, however, that complaining will not be an option at New Hope. We must face and confront every problem head-on and in a timely fashion. This is to be done in such a way that it honors the Lord and results in the building of biblical character.

8. We believe that the most effective evangelism happens through people inviting people.
We believe that a life will reach a life. Each believer develops genuine relationships with friends and family and extends an invitation to them. Evangelism gets to be a normal, natural lifestyle of winning others to Christ, one by one (see Prov. 11:30; John 1:43-45, 4:28-30).

The greatest evangelist is not Billy Graham, D. L. Moody or the pastor of some megachurch. The most effective evangelists are the individuals who make up the church. Every Christian has unchurched loved ones, friends or family members in need of the saving grace of Jesus Christ. Through these genuine relationships, a verbal witness is given or an invitation extended, and often an unchurched person becomes willing to investigate the claims of Christianity.

Sue Ann is a New Hope member on fire with the excitement of a new believer. I saw her seated at a table, at a Rotary convention, conversing with an elderly Japanese gentleman. Although she was much younger than he, they seemed to be old friends. I made my way over to greet her, and she introduced me to her friend. I can't remember his name, so we'll just call him "Mr. Miyagi."

"Mr. Miyagi, this is my pastor." Then, without a hiccup, she unfolded, in the most natural fashion, one of the finest and most memorable evangelistic campaigns I have ever witnessed.

"Mr. Miyagi," she said with a lilt, "do you go to church?"

"No," he replied. "I am a Buddhist."

"That's fine. But you *must* come to our church! Just come once, and your life will change. Mark my word!"

Mr. Miyagi, presuming she had misunderstood him, repeated his answer.

"No," he protested. "You see, I'm a Buddhist."

"That's fine!" she said optimistically. "But you just *have* to come to our church! Just once! Just come. You'll love it! You won't be the same."

"Well, I have my own religion," he said. "It's giving money to charitable organizations like the Boy Scouts and the United Way."

"That's fine," Sue Ann shot back, "but you just *have* to come to our church!"

"But I golf on Sundays," Mr. Miyagi finally admitted.

"That's fine, but you *must* come to our church!"

For the next 20 minutes, whatever reason he gave for his inability to accept her invitation, Sue Ann gave the same unwavering reply: "That's fine. Just come to our church. Just once. You'll never be the same!"

He could have said, "No, you see, I'm an alien from Alpha Centauri," and her reply would have remained the same: "That's fine, but you just have to come to our church. Come just once, and you'll never be the same!" I remember chuckling to myself and thinking, *You can't teach this kind of evangelism in Bible college. This comes straight from the heart!*

You see, when people feel excited about what God is doing in their church, evangelism becomes a natural by-product. Our eighth core value helps us keep this in mind. We know without a doubt that no ministry, program or event will win souls to Christ as effectively as a real, live person reaching out to another person, one-on-one.

The best form of evangelism is *Emmanuelism*, people recognizing that God is with us. And that can happen in gatherings of two and three family members, coworkers or friends—people who care enough to communicate Christ to the people in their lives. This value captures the heart of our church family.

9. We believe in identifying and training emerging leaders who are fully committed to Christ and who will reach their generation with the gospel.
God is raising up men and women who will take the baton of godly character, authentic faith and servant-hearted leadership into the next generation (see Ps. 78:6-7; 1 Tim. 3:1; 2 Tim. 2:2; Titus 1:5-9).

This core value constantly reminds us to give life away, to increase the base of leadership and to unselfishly live to make others successful. The ultimate test of a successful leader is not necessarily found in what he does, but rather, in what others are doing as a result of what he has done.

The Heart and Passion of New Hope

These core values, in tandem with our church's mission statement, make up the heart and passion of New Hope Christian Fellowship. We base all we do on them. We want our members to own these values so much that they permeate everything they do and say.

The heart and passion of New Hope make us unique. They are second in importance only to Jesus, for they compose the personality of our church, the very essence of our being. Without our heart and passion, we would be a set of dry doctrines, at best. With them, we have become a warm-hearted ministry, alive with God's love and passionate for His purposes.

If we were to alter our heart or passion in any way, we would be an altogether different church, for our expressed core values and mission establish our culture in every ministry and project we do.

Building a Common Culture

As alignment falls into place and those involved in your ministry catch the heart of its vision and core values, your church will begin to develop a common culture. Your overarching mission statement will direct your course and influence the thinking, actions and beliefs of every member, to the point that everyone believes, does and says the same things.

Let's say that a large supermarket hired you to stock the shelves. So you arrive at the specified time on your first day, and you and a few other workers are told to stock the canned goods. After a moment or two, you strike up a conversation: "How long you been working here?" you ask a fellow worker.

"About a year," he replies.

"I hired on just yesterday," you say. "I've never met the owner. What is it like to work here?"

Your coworker glares at you and gruffly says, "Just do your job and you won't have any problems. Keep your nose clean, your mouth shut and your eyes open. Pick up your paycheck and stay out of the customers' way. Got it?"

And so your first day begins. You now have an impression of the whole company, even before you meet the owner. Your fellow worker has established something of the corporate culture for you. By lunchtime, you're ready to check the classified ads for another job opportunity.

Let's try it again. It's your first day on the job and you strike up the same conversation with a coworker—except this time things go a bit differently.

"How long you been working here?" you ask.

"About a year," he replies.

"I hired on just yesterday. I've never met the owner. What kind of place is this to work at?"

Your coworker turns to you, smiles and says, "It's wonderful! I mean, the people here are like family to me. The owner is caring and interested in everyone. You'll absolutely love it! It won't be long before you will feel like family, too. Here, take a moment and let me introduce you to the other stock clerks."

And off you go with an entirely different feeling. Although you've never met the owner, you love the place. You have a feeling that you're going to enjoy working here.

Everyone in a church has the opportunity to share their culture with visitors and new members. How do church members, staff and volunteers know what their culture is? Typically they learn it through sermons, classes, teachings, personal relationships and small groups, all of which express the church's core values.

Culture can be defined as the way a church's members interact socially with one another; but in essence, its values reflect the basic tenets of their culture.

For example, a particular church might hold healthy relationships in high esteem, so you see this reflected in its core values. It might place a high value on evangelism, so the members focus on connecting every activity to a soul.

Such a church will tend to gear its weekend services to be easily understood by the average non-Christian. The music, drama and message feel modern, alive and relevant to what people go through every day. Even on the outside, members set up huge food and ministry tents in their courtyard. This all stems from the church's culture, the values its members hold dear.

A culture, then, is the sum of a church's heart—its core values in action. It's reflected in what it teaches and it bleeds into the way its members interact. (For more information about culture, see chapter 12.)

Finishing Well

About 30 years ago, an Olympic marathon went down in the annals of sports history, not for its greatness, but for its tragic ending.

The race started with the highest of hopes, each nation represented proudly by its best male runner, each athlete representing years of superhuman training and thousands of hours of running. These men were in their prime, the elite of their nations—literally the best of the best.

The starting gun fired, launching each man into a surge of muscular athleticism. Watching them sprint out of the blocks, you would never guess this race would cover more than 26 miles. Yet as the runners settled into their rhythmic pacing, the crowd settled in also, knowing that even the fastest man would not reach the finish life for at least another two hours. The marathon would end where it started, in front of grandstands full of spectators. In the meantime, the athletes ran their course outside the stadium, while other field events took place inside.

Two hours and four minutes later, the first returning runner came into view, and officials cleared the track. The runner led his rivals by a large margin, and the crowd cheered, straining to see him in the darkness of the tunnel leading into the stadium.

When he broke into the sunlight, the runner looked clearly delirious with exhaustion. He stumbled but quickly got back up. The cheering stadium fell silent. It appeared as though he had lost his sense of direction. He didn't know which way to go. His eyes had glazed over. Despite his obvious pain, he ran on.

Then he stopped again, looked around in a daze and started running the wrong way. One coach leaped from the stands to help him. "Get back," an Olympic official warned. "You can't touch him! If you touch him, that's it; he's disqualified. He'll be out of the race!" The coach stepped back, but the crowd began yelling directions to the runner. He still had a chance to win the gold and glory, because the other runners hadn't even come in sight yet. Yet despite the volume of an entire stadium crowd yelling, he felt too dazed to hear anything. He ran one way, looked around, ran the other way and finally fell down and just lay there.

The crowd leapt to its feet, urgently shouting, "Get up! Get up!" He struggled to stand and slowly stumbled to the finish, collapsing across the line. The crowd went crazy. Within minutes, the other runners entered the stadium and completed the race.

When the medals got handed out, however, the announcer shocked everyone by saying the fastest runner, the man who had beaten everyone else, had been disqualified. The reason? There were two finish lines: one line for sprints and the other, for the marathon. The "winner" ran to the wrong finish line! Prior to the race, he had been informed that the marathon runners would finish at the other end of the track; but because of his delirium, the runner forgot and finished at the wrong line. He had run superbly, apparently the best athlete that day—but because he lost his sense of direction, he lost it all. He didn't even place.

Think how much more tragic it would be if you ran hard your whole life, but finished poorly because you didn't accomplish what God asked you to accomplish. You didn't run the race set before you, and though you ran hard, you finished somebody else's race. As you cross the finish line, you may think, *Wow, look at that! The crowd is going bananas!*

And the Lord says, "But I asked you to run a different race. I equipped you to run a particular race."

You protest, "Yeah, but I ran this race, and everybody is so excited!"

In the end, though, the Lord is Judge; and only He can qualify or disqualify you, according to your obedience to His call. That's why Paul says, "I must consider everything else as nothing in order that I might finish well the race set before me" (see Acts 20:24).

Alignment is crucial to our finishing the race well. If you are a leader, make sure you catch God's vision for you and communicate it clearly to your people, that they might also run the race to win. Create an environment for effective ministry by setting the church's sights toward a common finish line and setting the church's heartbeat to a common culture through expressed values. When you do, you will find your people sharing a vibrant heart and a passion that fuels every step and every breath of every endeavor.

And you'll finish well!

Team Preparation

1. Write a definition of alignment. What does this mean for you and to your church?
2. Name some reasons for establishing core values early on in a ministry. What will these values help you to accomplish?

3. What are your church's core values? If you haven't written them down yet, think about the values your church holds dear—as reflected in its social, moral and intellectual practices—and then begin to record them.

4. How do you communicate your core values to the congregation? How often?

5. Can there be a difference between core values and culture? If so, how does that happen? How can this affect alignment?

C h a p t e r 1 1

BUILDING
TEAMS

*Our bodies have many parts, but the many parts make up only one
body when they are all put together. So it is with the "body" of Christ.*
1 CORINTHIANS 12:12, TLB

Doing church as a team is a whole new mind-set for many
churches today. But if we are going to be a church of the twenty-
first century, there's just no other way!

Often in the Bible, God refers to us as the Body of Christ.
The better we understand this metaphor, the more we will be
able to cooperate with God's design for His church.

The Church as a Body

The church is not an organization. It is more like an organism
with living parts that must move and work together as a whole.

An individual part cannot function on its own.

If I cut off my arm and plant it in dirt, that arm will not grow into a new body; it will die. So it is with the Body of Christ. Each of us has an individual assignment and role, but apart from the rest of the Body, we are useless. God created us that way. That is His design, not ours.

Have you ever noticed how each part of your physical body works in groups? For example, the hand works with five fingers, a palm, a wrist and forearm, with muscles, bones and tendons connecting them all. The integration of all these elements, working together, gives your composite hand and forearm agility and coordination. Every part of your body works best as a team, with all of its parts serving in harmony and cooperating toward a common goal.

Have you ever watched a concert pianist move his fingers in perfect synchronization, running arpeggios up and down the keys of a piano? Each sinew, each ligament, every finger, muscle and joint work together to create a symphony of notes blended together in beautiful harmony. No one finger, by itself, could accomplish what the score calls for. The wrist can't do it alone, and neither can the arm. But by working together, each part fulfilling its role, they can fill a concert hall with magnificent music that enthralls an audience and sets hearts soaring.

This is the church—connected to "the Head, that is, Christ" (Eph. 4:15, *NIV*) and working together for the "common good" (1 Cor. 12:7). Each of us is to be a living, functioning, serving member of the Body of Christ. God has gifted each of us with talents and abilities. He has divinely endowed us with all we need to serve His purposes—and we do this best in teams.

Building teams does not begin with a certain kind of technique; it begins with a certain kind of heart—an unselfish, authentic heart, desiring only God's best. Such a heart constantly asks, *How can I include others?* It anticipates the joy of sharing experiences, struggles and victories, realizing that, like the body, we work best in teams—the way God designed us to function.

The Beginnings of Fractal Team Building

I owe much of the understanding of this metaphor to a longtime friend, Loren Cunningham, founder and former president of Youth With A Mission. I met Loren for the first time in Hilo decades ago. Loren is a big man, standing over six feet tall. I remember the first time I shook his hand. Mine disappeared in his, and I felt secretly glad to get it back.

Well, his heart is as big as he is.

A few summers ago, Loren visited Hawaii. We were having lunch together in Waikiki on a balmy Sunday afternoon. During the meal, I asked Loren if he would share some ideas he had garnered along the way on equipping God's people to reach the lost. That one question ignited three hours of brisk interchange and conversation.

That day Loren shared with me a seed thought about *fractal patterns*, which he had heard Winkey Pratney discuss in a seminar. We sat and talked until it looked like our waiter was about to charge us double for loitering.

This process for building teams is by no means the only way. Dozens of time-tested ways to build teams exist, and no one way is necessarily the best. Find one that works best for you and do it! The bottom line is this: *You can't do it alone.* You weren't designed to. What you will read in these next few pages is a way that works well for us at New Hope Community Church. We're still hammering it out, but it works splendidly with our style and makeup.

The Church: A Living Organism

According to *Webster's Dictionary*, the word "fractal" means "any of various extremely irregular curves or shapes for which any suitably chosen part is similar in shape to a given larger or smaller part when magnified or reduced to the same size."[1]

If you're anything like me, you're just as much in the dark after reading this definition as you were before. Let me see if I can explain it as it pertains to doing church as a team.

Living organisms are, in many aspects, quite similar to organizations, while in other ways they are very different. Both require structure, direction, measurable objectives and leadership. On the other hand, an organism is a living entity with emotions, changes, natural growth and a susceptibility to disease, accidents, predators and sicknesses.

The church, or the Body of Christ, is a living organism. It may have organizational needs, but organization alone would make it unhealthy. Like a silk plant, the church could look fine on the outside but remain lifeless on the inside. Silk plants often impress from a distance, but up close, you can tell they have no life and no fragrance.

Sometimes it seems easier to treat the church as an organization because, like silk plants, once they get arranged, they seem to require little maintenance. They might look good—but don't get too close! Recall once more the fig tree described in the book of Mark: "And seeing at a distance a fig tree in leaf, He went to see if perhaps He would find anything on it; and when He came to it, He found nothing but leaves" (Mark 11:13). Jesus actually cursed the fig tree, causing it to wither overnight. The tree looked good from a distance, but up close it lacked any evidence of fruit.

If you are looking for a low-maintenance structure, fractals and teams will not suit you. Anything living requires maintenance. Silk plants look pretty, but they cannot bear fruit. Living things require your attention. A church is just like a marriage; unmaintained, it dies. (My wife often reminds me of this sentence.) If we want this team to live and bear much fruit, we can't avoid the high maintenance it requires.

The Repeating Pattern

The fractal design for doing church as a team resembles the pattern in living organisms more than anything I have seen. Despite the unwieldy origins of the name, it's a simple concept that works. Simply put, it's a structure that repeats itself over and over again.

Take the fern, for example. Here in Hawaii, these plants grow everywhere. If you look at the fern plant in its entirety, you will see one major stem with smaller branches extending on either side. Now, take a closer look at one of the branches. You will see the same structure duplicated, with a major stem and smaller leaves extending. If your eyesight is good, observe closely one of the individual leaves. You will see that very same structure duplicated again, with a major vein running down the middle of the leaf and several more extending from it. If you had a microscope, you could see that structure duplicated again and again on an even smaller scale.

Our bodies have a similar fractal design. We see one major unit, called the trunk, with limbs extending. Take one of the limbs and within it you'll see a major artery with several others branching off from it. Then take one of the secondary arteries and you will again see several more branching off, until they supply every area of the body with blood, thus making possible good circulation and good health.

Doing church as a team uses this fractal design—a very simple, repeating pattern found in most organisms. Each unit has similar patterns and similar purposes.

For the sake of simplicity, we build our teams in groupings of five. It seems to work best for providing the care each person in the group needs, but also for another reason.

By Exodus 18, Moses was burning out. He carried an excruciating load, and the weight was killing him. Jethro, his father-in-law, saw his predicament and gave him counsel: "You will surely wear out, both yourself and these people who are with you, for the task is too heavy for you; you cannot do it alone" (v. 18). Then he gave Moses the remedy in verse 21: "Furthermore, you shall select out of all the people able men who fear God, men of truth, those who hate dishonest gain; and you shall place these over them as leaders of thousands, of hundreds, of fifties and of tens."

The smallest grouping was 10—the same advice we take in deciding on our smallest team. It is not 1 person, but 10. How does this play out?

Let's say I have a passion to work with kids, and I have some teaching gifts and organizational skills. Someone asks me to help with the children's ministry, so I say yes.

In doing church as a team, I do not first jump in and start working with the children. Instead, I build a team of 4 other leaders. When I choose the 4, we have a team totaling 5 people, with similar passions and supportive gifts. But then I add an "X" in each box for that person's spouse (or if one or more of my teammates is single, to remind me of *relationships*). With an "X" next to each person, we have a team of 10, the smallest group size in Exodus 18.

I work with a fractal team of 4 others, and each one of those team members has outside relationships. Are they healthy or unhealthy? I am committed not just to each person, but I also want their primary relationships to remain healthy. If one of my core leaders struggles at home, do you think it will affect his ministry at church? Absolutely! Fractals cannot work without healthy relationships (more about this in chapter 13).

If you were asked to oversee and lead the children's ministry, how would you build a team? Well, let's say that the age range in our children's ministry will be from newborns through fourth graders. So we form our teams: (1) nursery and toddlers; (2) prekindergarten and kindergarten; (3) first and second grade, and; (4) third and fourth grade. The following graph illustrates this fractal building process:

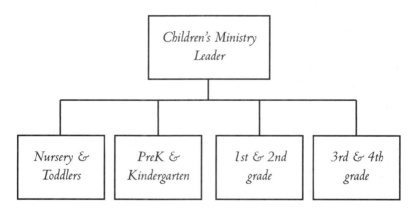

Using the fractal design, I find a person who loves babies. When this nursery and toddler leader agrees to become part of the children's ministry team, he or she does not immediately jump in and start working with babies. Instead, duplicating the pattern of what just happened, the nursery leader builds a team of four other leaders with similar passions and supporting gifts. So another team gets built to serve the nursery and toddlers.

Here's an example of how it might look when the nursery and toddler leader builds a team:

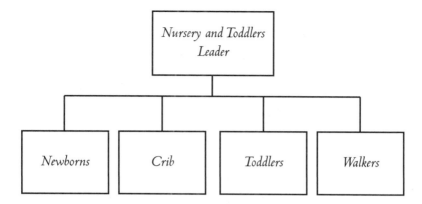

Each of the other leaders—prekindergarten and kinder-garten, first and second grade team and the third and fourth grade team—does exactly the same thing, duplicating the team-building process.

Then, if you add up all the teams, the four main leaders each serving with four on their individual teams, the leadership of the children's ministry grows immediately to 21 people (of course, always remembering the importance of healthy relationships!). And that's going just two deep. This pattern can be continued by building out to a third or even a fourth level. As large as the ministry grows, the teams simply grow deeper.

With this pattern of ministry, growth occurs downward. That is, the larger the ministry grows, the deeper the levels of teams you build. For example, if the nursery and toddler team has its four leaders (Newborns, Crib, Toddlers and Walkers) and the Lord increases the ministry threefold, then what do we do? Relax! We no longer need to stress or burn the midnight oil of worry. In the fractal design, the leader of the newborns finds four other leaders, and they each do the very same thing. Each chooses four new leaders with similar passions and sup-portive gifts to form another level of leadership. Growth occurs downward:

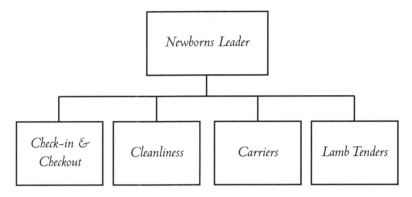

This can go on indefinitely, and you can get as creative as needed. In this way, every person stays included, and every person has a role to fill. But remember, regardless of how large the ministry grows, God will always provide the servants necessary for the assignment.

Growth Without Burnout

Consider another wonderful aspect of this design. As the leader of the children's ministry, I will serve primarily with four other leaders: the nursery and toddler leader, the prekindergarten and kindergarten leader, the first and second grade leader, and the third and fourth grade leader. These four people make up my team. But what happens when the ministry grows? How many leaders will I personally oversee?

Four. (Again, remember the "relationships" mind-set.)

What if the ministry doubles and we have to increase our leadership base by two more levels? How many people will I personally oversee if the ministry grows from 10 nursery-age children to 100?

Four.

What if it grows to 200?

Still four.

That's right. The answer will always be four! Each leader will always oversee four others. This way, no one burns out. You care for four people (or a team of five plus relationships with five others).

At New Hope, growth is always downward. The larger the ministry, the deeper the leadership base goes.

Natural Discipleship Groupings

This design also shows its genius in that each team falls into natural groupings of five. These can become discipleship groups, each formed because of similar passions and paths of ministry. This may be the easiest and simplest way to begin a small-groups ministry at your church.

By seeing your leaders as your small group, the common tasks become much more than a responsibility to be fulfilled. The group leader can care for and nurture each person individually. Likewise, each of the four leaders will have their own groups of four. In this way, each person gets nurtured while they themselves nurture four others.

With the fractal design, our church becomes not a church with small groups, but a church of small groups. Here, people in a small group are accountable to their leader, and that leader is accountable to another leader. Each person disciples others as well as gets discipled.

Simplifying the Design

In math class I learned to boil everything down to its lowest common denominator. I understand everything more clearly when I can see it in its simplest form, so that's what we did at New Hope. Using the principles of fractal leadership, we simplified the form so that we could teach it to our teams. This one idea is foundational to everything we do.

Whether you are beginning a new ministry or taking part in an existing one, understanding the team-building process will help. I like to use pictures, so here's how I present the fractal design.

Step One: DRAW A CIRCLE
The first step in building your team, whether you're starting a new ministry or building another level into an existing one, is always the same. Begin by drawing a circle.

Draw a Circle.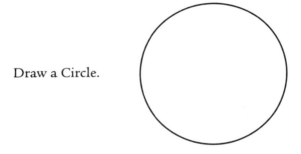

That's it. Draw a circle. This circle represents the parameters of your ministry. In concept, this is everything for which you will be responsible.

If you oversee the children's ministry, this circle embraces everything connected to that ministry. If you are a senior pastor, this represents everything about your church and its ministry: the services, pastoral care, leadership, counseling, discipleship, finances, organization, facilities and more—in other words, *everything*. If you are a volunteer overseeing the ushering ministry, this might include the passing out of bulletins, seating people and seeing to their needs. If you are a volunteer who directs the hospitality ministry, this circle will represent everything that the hospitality ministry includes, whether known or as yet unknown.

At this point, you may not know everything that belongs within this circle. But don't worry! You'll discover its contents along the way. This simply sets the parameters, or boundaries, of your role.

Step Two: CROSSHAIRS

Second, draw a cross in the middle of your circle. Picture it as if you were looking through the viewfinder of a camera or the scope of a rifle. The circle should now resemble the crosshairs in the lens. This shows you what you are aiming at—exactly what this step is meant to accomplish.

Draw a Cross Within a Circle.

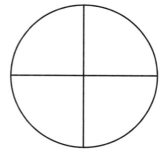

Write down your aim or the purpose for your ministry. What is its intention, its God-glorifying purpose? Each ministry within the church should clearly and precisely know its purpose. Keep in mind the heart of the Great Commission, along with the church's overarching mission statement. Then, in one or two sentences, articulate why you are embarking on this venture.

What is the goal of this ministry? What should it accomplish that will put it in sync with the overall direction of the church?

Consider a few mission statements, or aims, at New Hope:

Front Lines Ministries

To present the gospel of Jesus Christ in such a way that

turns non-Christians into converts—in contemporary ways that reach the heart.

Midweek LEAD Services

To develop committed disciples of Jesus Christ through passionate worship, in-depth study of God's Word and dynamic prayer.

New Hope Resources Ministry

To be a source of supply and support that builds up the Body of Christ within, and to provide tools to reach out for the furtherance of the Great Commission.

Missions

Extending the heart of New Hope beyond Hawaii's borders for evangelism and equipping.

Graphic Arts Ministry

Equipping the church with excellent and effective visual tools for communicating the gospel of Jesus Christ.

This step is crucial in doing church as a team. It gives everyone the same starting point for understanding how everything fits together. Without this step, individuals and individual ministries will build from different sets of blueprints. Then, regardless of how sincere or how hard each one tries, expectations will inevitably collide.

Some ministries spend more of their time putting out personality fires than in doing the ministry. Why? Because they inadvertently aim at different targets. They must identify their purpose up front. The clearer the target, the better the chance of hitting it!

Step Three: TITLE QUADRANTS

The next step begins by asking a few questions:

- If this ministry (or project or responsibility) were broken into four separate quadrants, what would they be?
- What would I call each one?
- Would the combination of these four encapsulate the total responsibilities for fulfilling this ministry?

Title each quadrant of your circle with a heading that describes its purpose. The combination of these four should match the purpose statement you have just written. Likewise, your purpose statement should align with the overall purpose statement for the church. (At the end of this chapter, the study questions will help you to practice these steps.)

The circle that encompasses the whole ministry of New Hope Christian Fellowship looks something like this:

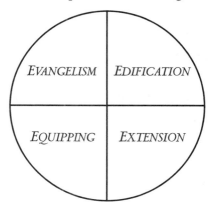

EVANGELISM | *EDIFICATION*

EQUIPPING | *EXTENSION*

Step Four: GIFTS NECESSARY

Fourth, determine what gifts or gift mix would make the best fit for a person overseeing each quadrant. Would the gift of evangelism be necessary for someone serving as a leader in outreach events? Absolutely.

What about temperament? Would this person need to be a task-oriented individual, or more of a people-oriented person? Would this person best fit the task if he or she were an introvert? An extrovert?

All aspects of a person's DESIGN should be taken into consideration to find the best possible fit.

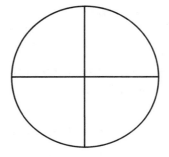

Determine What Gifts Are Required Within Each Quadrant.

Just as a reminder, let's take a look at the distinction between an introvert and an extrovert. An extrovert loves people; just being with them charges his batteries. When isolated from others, his batteries drain. An introvert also loves people, but being with them tends to drain his batteries. He has to periodically isolate himself to get recharged.

Although I tend to be an introvert, I share many qualities with extroverts. I need time alone to recharge my batteries, but my batteries drain very slowly when I am with people. And if I am isolated for an extended length of time, I go stir crazy.

In the sixth grade, for example, I lived with my family in Japan. I attended a small military school in a town called Sagamihara. Miss Anne Clifford was my sixth-grade teacher—as tall as the school flagpole and as mean as they come. From time to time, she disciplined me (no doubt for some silly, unfair and concocted reason). She did so by confining me to the coat closet for 15 minutes per each trumped-up charge.

I could tolerate sitting in the dark for the first five minutes, but at that point in my incarceration, I'd start to go crazy. I would rather she had tortured me with bamboo splinters under my fingernails. When I couldn't stand it any longer, I'd begin pacing the floor, counting the number of boards from one end to the other. Next I would try on all the coats, scrounge through the pockets for any leftover candy, or switch one kid's boots with another kid's coat, making new and curious combinations.

Although I'm an introvert, I *have* to be with people. I hate being cooped up alone. I have to fellowship, talk and be with others.

In the same way, God knows your design, and He wants to match your internal makeup with your ministry, your temperament with your tasks. God knew my design; that's the reason I am the way I am. If you don't like the way I am, don't blame me. It's God's fault! (You may laugh here.)

Step Five: NAMES

In this step, identify the individuals who might fit the required gift combinations. Ask yourself who in your congregation would be the best for the job. Talk to those who may know or who may have seen these individuals in action. Do your best to fit the names with the gifts required, the temperament needed and the maturity necessary for the task or position in question.

When you complete this step well, you increase the chances for each chosen leader to enjoy a lasting and fruitful experience in ministry.

Step Six: ASK

Finally, *ask*. Don't wait for volunteers to magically appear, uniformed and ready for duty. Challenge the men and women whom you think would fit. Since you've already done the research, many of those you ask may actually feel excited to sign up!

God has someone for each ministry He initiates, so don't force pieces into the wrong slots by not doing your homework. Guard yourself from the temptation to fill a position with a warm body. Follow the process; it will spare you many pains later on.

But *ask,* especially if you genuinely feel that you may release someone's dream. It will astonish you to see what you can accomplish simply by asking. Not only will you often receive what you ask for, but many times the other person will thank you for taking the initiative!

Jesus did this. He asked. He found some potential disciples and asked each of them to "Come, follow me" (Mark 1:17, *NIV*). Jesus further instructs us to ask the Father for what we need: "Ask, and it shall be given to you; seek, and you shall find; knock, and it shall be opened to you" (Matt. 7:7).

Here's a key to asking someone to join up: You must be completely authentic in your invitation. You must sincerely believe that you want to see that person grow and be used in wonderful ways by the Holy Spirit.

Sometimes our fear causes us to shy away from asking. We fret about the outcome. We worry that we might offend or bother people, or that they might perceive us as needy or weak. Perhaps worse, they might perceive us as attempting to take advantage of our relationship with them. Relax! On the contrary, it is actually quite arrogant and self-righteous to assume that others aren't willing to help or assist. They may be *waiting* for the invitation!

You Need Others

One final reminder as we close this chapter. I am sure that you are a nice person and very capable—but, quite frankly, you *need* people in ministry. You cannot develop the perfect ministry on your own. You cannot come up with every creative idea yourself.

Plenty of others are as gifted (if not more so) than you. And plenty of others are willing to pitch in and offer their expertise, advice and assistance.

When I get together with some of our staff and we gang up to tackle a problem, there's nothing we can't solve! Moreover, my colleagues spark all kinds of new ideas in me. And that, friends, is when my creative juices *really* start to flow!

Team Preparation

Practice building a team by following each of these steps:

1. What is the first step?
2. Next, draw the circle with crosshairs in it. What do the crosshairs represent?

   Write out the aim or purpose of the team you are building.
3. Next, title your four quadrants.
   a. Quadrant one:
   b. Quadrant two:
   c. Quadrant three:
   d. Quadrant four:
4. List the gifts necessary for being a leader in each quadrant.
   a.
   b.
   c.
   d.
5. Write the names of possible leaders for each of these quadrants.

a.

b.

c.

d.

6. Are you an introvert or an extrovert? On the continuum below, place an X where you think you fall.

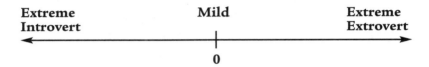

7. Covering up the graph above, ask a friend or spouse to place an X on the graph below where they believe you fall.

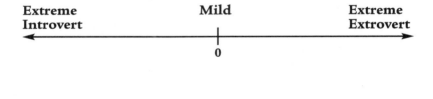

Note

1. *Merriam-Webster's Collegiate Dictionary*, 10th ed., s.v. "fractal."

TRANSITIONING A CHURCH CULTURE

These stones shall become a memorial to the sons of Israel forever.

JOSHUA 4:7

We visited Travis in the juvenile detention holding. Like many other high school students incarcerated in this dreary place, Travis had entered a chemical dependency program to dry out.

He had recently given his life to Christ and had begun to grow in his newfound faith. After six months in juvie, finally the day of his discharge had come. We felt excited about his new beginning and his fresh start. He could go home, faith-filled and free from the nagging pull of drugs.

"I can't go home," he told me. "I'm *not* going back home."

"What!?" I objected. "Travis, you can return home. You're *free*. God has given you a new beginning!"

"If you send me home," he warned, "I will run away again."

"But why?" I asked incredulously.

"Because it was at home that I picked up the habit," he explained. "My parents do drugs at our house. They deal the stuff, and if I go home, I will get back into it all over again. God has done a great thing in me, and I am free. I have to stay that way—and if I go home, I won't be able to."

Chalk it up to yet another terrible home environment.

Travis knew the right things, read the right books, took the right classes and knew what drugs could do to him. Yet he also knew that if he returned to the same unhealthy environment that had sent him to rehab, he could kiss any further growth good-bye. And he refused to let that happen.

I think a lot of churches could learn from his determination.

Making the Switch

Every church has a specific culture. It may not be written down, but it definitely gets expressed in everything that happens. It bleeds into every activity and decision. It colors every perspective and directs every destiny.

But what if that culture is unhealthy, unwholesome, even toxic? Or what if it's just not as healthy as you wish it were? How do you go about changing a mediocre or deficient culture that has existed for years? How do you transition a traditional ministry, destined for decline, and turn it into a vibrant and healthy spiritual juggernaut? Where do you find the alchemy that changes a one-man show into a team-based ministry?

I have no silver bullet or magic elixir. But I have seen dozens of traditional churches transition into wonderfully healthy, team-based ministries. I know of no golden keys, but I can suggest several principles that will help guide you on your way.

Know What You Want

The first step is to understand that healthy church cultures don't happen automatically. You have to know what it is that you want to grow—what does it look like? What does it produce? How does it differ from other options out there?—and then take specific action to cultivate the kind of growth that you want to see take place.

If you let a plot of ground bear whatever it wants to, you'll end up with a tangled patch of weeds. If you want apple trees, you have to decide that's what you want, from the very beginning. Then you grow apple trees and remove anything that isn't an apple tree. You don't merely *wish* for an apple orchard; you *cultivate* the orchard.

In many ways, this first step mirrors how God tells us to cultivate our personal thought life. Left to themselves, our thoughts scatter in a lot of directions, many of which are distinctly unhealthy and even ungodly. If you want to grow healthy fruit in the garden of your mind, and not noxious weeds, then you have to first identify what good thoughts look like. Once you know that, then you cultivate those thoughts and uproot anything that doesn't match the target description. Paul said it like this:

> Finally, brothers, whatever is true, whatever is noble, whatever is right, whatever is pure, whatever is lovely, whatever is admirable—if anything is excellent or praiseworthy—think about such things (Phil. 4:8, *NIV*).

If something pops into your head that doesn't fit this

description—if it looks impure rather than pure, for example, or worthless rather than admirable—then you rip it out and refuse to let it take up space in the garden of your mind. It's a battle! Don't think that it isn't. In another place, the apostle wrote,

> We demolish arguments and every pretension that sets itself up against the knowledge of God, and *we take captive every thought to make it obedient to Christ* (2 Cor. 10:5, *NIV*, emphasis added).

Demolition takes work. Capturing enemy patrols takes vigilance and clear vision. And to accomplish either one, you first have to know what the good guys look like and what the bad guys look like. Otherwise, you might end up demolishing the wrong pillboxes and capturing the wrong patrols.

Transitioning a church from one model to another takes exactly this kind of careful foresight, vigilance, and action. You have to know both what you'd like to see in your church *and* what you don't want anywhere near it. So ask yourself a few simple questions:

- What about our church do I like?
- What about our church draws people to it?
- What aspects of our church look like weeds?
- What aspects of our church turn off visitors?

Pray about these questions; don't merely throw out a few answers off the top of your head. Ask God what *He* thinks. Ask Him to identify for you both the fruit and the weeds that may be growing in your church, and then ask Him to help you develop a specific list of traits that He'd like to see blooming in your church's garden.

Invisible Megaphones

I lived for three years in Japan, and since that time have traveled there extensively. One winter, my wife and I took an extended tour into the smaller, more remote villages in the countryside of Japan's beautiful land.

We often saw huge stones adorned with writing, standing at the entrances of small villages. Each of these huge stones loomed above us like monolithic sentinels, reminding us—no, *warning* us—of certain things required of all who entered. On each stone we saw etched different *kanji*, or Chinese characters, like nameplates on a soldier's chest.

Heian, or "peace," one invisible megaphone instructed all who entered. *Chikara*, or "strength," another declared. A third weighed in with the word *Gamman*, or "perseverance."

These stony elders stood day and night to remind all who lived there—and all who entered—the values that this particular village held in high esteem.

Eskimo elders did something similar. They built *totems* to display their values, each prominently diplayed with an identifiable icon, such as an animal, to represent the village's values. They carved these totems onto a *totem pole*, which might display a bear for strength, a salmon to represent perseverance, a fox for cunning, or the elk for vigilance. They then placed the totem pole in the middle of the village to silently instruct and remind every villager of the values and ideals that held them together.

The Bible reminds us that God instructed the ancient Israelites to engage in a very similar practice. He told our patriarchs of faith to display certain values that not only encouraged learning but also cultivated an atmosphere where these values were diplayed, lived out and maintained.

Through a miraculous parting of waters—not unlike the more famous Red Sea miracle accomplished in Moses' day—

Joshua took his Hebrew warriors over the Jordan River to capture Jericho. But even before he stepped foot on the dry riverbed, God instructed him to erect a memorial on the other side of the Jordan to remind future generations of certain values the people of God were always to hold in high esteem.

> When your children ask later, saying, "What do these stones mean to you?" then you shall say to them, "Because the waters of the Jordan were cut off before the ark of the covenant of the Lord; when it crossed the Jordan, the waters of the Jordan were cut off"; So these stones shall become a memorial to the sons of Israel forever. (Joshua 4:6-7).

In other words, if you want to encourage the building of a certain culture, you can help it along by creating certain visible reminders of what that culture should look like.

We change a church culture in much the same way that the elders of a village shape theirs. Consider five steps in transitioning a church culture:

- Identify biblical totems
- Discuss it with the leaders until it resounds
- To change things, tell them what will not change
- Display totems for all to see
- Choose the oak over the squash

Identify Biblical Totems

The elders of a church must decide which biblical values they most want the ministry to incarnate. These totems will shape the culture of the ministry over the ensuing years.

At New Hope Christian Fellowship, this took place only after a few years of ministry. I asked myself and our leaders the following set of questions:

- What are we known for?
- Are these the things we *want* to be known for?
- Are these values biblical?
- Will these remain relevant in the next generation?
- Can we dedicate ourselves to unreservedly live out these values?

Once I knew the answers to these questions, I began writing what came to be known as New Hope's totems. Each church will have differing values that it holds as important—and so long as they remain biblical, no values are right or wrong; they simply identify your culture, the spirit with which you carry out your God-given assignment and the tenor in which you make decisions and plan your activities.

Consider these totems as cousins to your core values; the two will and should overlap. The major difference between the two is that the core values are more general and overarching. It's the totems that we specifically emphasize. They keep us tethered to the foundational values that create culture.

At New Hope, we emphasize the following totems:

1. An Undying Devotion to God and His Word

This totem has helped to cultivate one of the traits that identify the DNA of our church. From the formulation of our *Life Journals* to our Pacific Rim Bible College, this totem has served as the compass for many of our key decisions. Thousands of Life Groups (and I mean that literally) meet each week, where hungry men and women eagerly sit at the Master's feet, listening to His Word.

The Bible has become our policy manual, our employee handbook, our supervisor's guidelines, and the map that corrects our course. If one single thing has improved the health of our church and spurred its growth, it is the self-feeding program of a systematic study of His Word.

2. A Dedication to Evangelism

Everything we do is connected to a soul. Whether we're setting up a speaker or teaching Sunday School, we see everything as a means to helping a person to get to know Christ. We realize that we have but one life to give for our Master, and it will soon be over. This is a totem dear to our souls and it marks the personality of our ministry. New Hope is a harvest church.

This totem hangs in the air. It bleeds into everything we do, even though we don't necessarily have programs and classes in personal evangelism. Evangelism is part of our culture, and when a totem is just part of the culture, it happens almost instinctively. Culture allows core values to become a natural expression of the church, rather than a programmed response.

3. A Gracious Spirit in All Our Dealings

We will face many setbacks and much opposition, but the setbacks will never be eternal; that's reserved for the *spirit* with which we respond to the setbacks. People remember how their leaders dealt with the problem and how they treated the people involved, much longer than they recall the problem itself. So, determined to cultivate a gracious spirit, we strive to remain unwavering in His ways and true to His very best.

Being gracious does not mean we are gullible; we know we must remain aware and vigilant. We do not equate grace with leniency, or love with being nice. Being gracious means we maintain an unshakable faith in the midst of storms and we do not let an outside storm become an inside storm. It means holding fast to God's ways while understanding that we will always be dealing with wounded people for whom Christ died.

4. An Atmosphere of Learning

New Hope has cultivated an environment of learning and growing. Even though it might be easier to let things slide, we realize that to do so would allow wrong habits to solidify, thus forfeiting future character. We debrief *everything* so that we might move constantly toward improvement. This doesn't mean striving for perfection, but rather choosing an attitude that cultivates a spirit of excellence. Constant feedback, mixed with healthy portions of encouragement and celebration, makes for a tasty recipe for growth.

This begins with leaders who willingly remain open to discussion and instruction. We want to create an atmosphere in which it feels normal to make one another successful. In such an environment, no one is autonomous. And since we live to make each other successful, we cannot do so without a culture of learning.

5. Healthy, Genuine Relationships

Every church deals with people: broken people, immature people, hurt people, selfish people, even deranged people. But we recognize that the first step to healing is to trust those who speak into our lives.

I'll say more about this in the next chapter, but healthy relationships are vital to doing church as a team. We cannot allow any unresolved conflicts to go underground. Relational bitterness or tolerated unforgiveness will sour even a healthy culture. When disagreements and misunderstandings occur—and they do, all the time—this totem reminds us that the relationship is more important than the particular task at hand. And when things do go bad in a relationship, this totem insists that repairing and maintaining friendships in the church helps us to develop a culture of fruitfulness.

6. Live Heart First

In the beginning, we pioneered the ministry of New Hope with little resources, few people, and a dozen chairs—but with tons of heart! That's really all we had—*heart!* But God found it sufficient for His purposes. We watched Him take that one ingredient and, through it, accomplish miracles.

As the months flew by, we noticed the heart disappearing. Our activities grew, our programs increased, and our chairs filled up. Professional musicians began to attend and blend into our music teams. We held great services and lots of activities— but the tasks eventually began to outpace the hearts.

One symptom of a shrinking heart is that people begin to burn out. They get tired and discouraged. Once-visible leaders slowly become transparent and eventually disappear, to be replaced by leaders with more zeal but less depth. Talent overshadows heart—and if we are not careful, we can see it as a fair exchange.

It's time to get back to heart.

We pruned back a few activities. Think of it as cutting back an overgrown hedge in an effort to showcase the gate it once adorned.

We pruned back until we could once again see the heart of our people. What God used in the beginning to grow the church is what He will still use today—people who live *heart first.*

After a season of outstanding musicals and delightful services at New Hope, we decided to have a night of music and feature our very best. The lighting rivaled a Broadway musical and the band sounded as if it had stepped straight out of an appearance at the Dove Awards.

And then it happened. I am not sure how it happened, but I am glad it did.

A Down's syndrome girl stepped up to the stage to perform a sign dance to the popular chorus by Darlene Zschech "Shout to the Lord." Her innocent heart and her genuine devotion left no dry eye in the auditorium. Never before or since have I seen such a beautiful, authentic expression of praise.

Then I heard the Lord whisper: "I have silenced all of heaven and commanded everyone's attention while she danced. I heard her heart, and that is the most beautiful sound in the Kingdom."

Each season that passes, I watch our heart. Is it obvious? Is it genuine? Whenever we need to, we correct back to heart. No, we don't prune simply because we have too many activities. We prune until we see each activity fueled by genuine hearts, unabashed hearts, in love with Jesus Christ.

That's when heaven comes down and glory fills our souls.

Discuss It with the Leaders Until It Resounds

Each ministry must decide what it wants to grow in its garden and identify the plants that it wants to become fruitful. The previous six totems are not exhaustive, but they give New Hope enough dots that, when connected, enable us to begin to create a healthy culture.

Sit with some leaders in your ministry and discuss your totems. What should they be for you? Be sure that they are biblical and contextual to your church and community. They should identify the "you" that would delight our Father.

Let me caution you, however: Leaders are not only the culture-setters, they can also be the vilest of culture-breakers! So much rises and falls on spiritual leadership. Each leader, each elder, helps to shape tomorrow's church. Leaders hold in their hands the DNA of the next generation. It's not too much to say that the church of tomorrow will become what we are today!

Why do I say this? I say it because *you can teach what you know, but in the end, you will reproduce what you are.*

Remember that line. Let it sink in. It has held true over my many years of consulting with churches and watching the ebb and flow of ministries. Leaders and elders must buy into the culture you want to produce, because we will reproduce not what we believe, but what we are.

Let the leaders, the elders, the major players and the influencers all weigh in on these totems. Whether it takes a month or a year, do not pass "GO," do not collect $200, until you finish this. The leaders will set the culture, maintain the values, or destroy them.

Each totem must be practiced and lived until it becomes natural. At New Hope, I do not announce anything formally until I see these values bleeding out of our leaders in everyday settings. Their conversation, their teaching, their discussions all reveal healthy helpings of these values. This is a season of "practice." It may take a year or more until daily devotions become a lived-out-loud value. And then we make it a totem.

The great cellist, Yo-Yo Ma, is renown not only for his technical expertise but also for the emotional sensitivity that marks his playing. In an interview, he described the importance of practicing until the music moves past the notes and into one's heart. He reminded aspiring cellists to practice not until they have achieved technical proficiency but until the technical proficiency disappears. At that stage, a performer begins to play, not only with a high degree of skill, but from the heart.

When these totems get lived out naturally in the leadership, I say that the church has become *pregnant.*

And then what's the next natural step? Why, birth, of course.

To Change Things, Tell Them What Will Not Change

Nobody likes change, although we all know that growth requires change. None of us wants the opposite of growth. When a tree stops growing, there's a scientific term for this condition. It's called *dead!*

But really, it's not *change* that people dislike. It is abrupt change, unnecessary change, painful change, disruptive change, and poorly orchestrated change. If done well, change can be accepted and even welcomed, even by the stodgiest of them all.

Music is like that. If the arranger does his homework and the musicians play their parts well, a song can modulate from key to key without disrupting the song; the change only enhances the performance.

Shifting a culture and transitioning a church can follow a similar track, as long as the arrangers do their homework and the leaders do their part. When it's done right, the congregation might not even realize that the chords have changed and the notes have been moved; they welcome the change and appreciate the more beautiful song.

Let's assume you've discussed the totems and agreed on

some biblical ones. The leaders have practiced them into lifestyle until it bleeds out of their hearts. A year, maybe two, goes by. Now you want to go public—but how?

To change things, tell the people what will never change. In other words, if evangelism is one of your new totems, don't start by telling everyone that they have to start sharing Christ. Don't tell them how the church has failed in this area, and it's high time we changed the downward trend. No one likes to dig out from holes!

> *To change things, tell the people what will never change.*

Instead, tell them what won't ever change. Believe that in each heart beats a dedication to God and His Word, otherwise they would not be sitting in church. Start there. Then tell them, with evangelism in mind, what will never change. Keep it positive and motivating. You might say something like this:

> I am so honored to have the privilege of leading this great church that has been here so faithfully for 100 years. What an honor that God has seen fit for us to continue His great work for this long in this community! This loving, God-fearing church has a marvelous heritage that has left us a wonderful example to follow. In fact, every one of us is here because someone in the past

has prayed for you, invited you, cared for you. We have a great heritage! And that cannot change as we move into our new year.

In fact, what must never change is our love for people who live apart from the things of God, just as each one of us did at one time. What must never change in our church is a heart for those kinds of people. We cannot, we must not, drift from what we stand for—evangelism!

Do you see what just happened? You modulated the song, and no one noticed! All they know is that you have honored their church's past and that they cannot change what was set in place long ago.

Nobody likes change, but everyone likes to grow. Present the transition in such a way that you help people to realize their own dreams.

Display Totems for All to See

Speak to the sons of Israel, and tell them that they shall make for themselves tassels on the corners of their garments throughout their generations . . . for you to look at and remember all the commandments of the Lord, so as to do them and not follow after your own heart and your own eyes (Num. 15:38-39).

We all have a tendency to forget. We are prone to it, and God knows our unfortunate tendency. For good reason, the apostle Peter tells us, "I will always remind you of these things, even though you know them and are firmly established in the truth you now have" (2 Pet. 1:12). Since we have a tendency to forget,

God takes steps to help us remember.

In the Old Testament, God gave His people specific instructions in remembering. He called them tassels.

Tassels were simply lengths of cord or material that extended down from the corners of a robe, each one reminding the wearer of a commandment of God. In this way, each person would recall what God had said; with each step, a swaying tassel would remind them of some particular divine commandment.

We have tassels, too. In our homes, we may have a Scripture verse artistically framed on a wall. We might have a picture of a recent trip with the church group, or something that points us back to God's provision or goodness. These are simple reminders, appropriately displayed, to recall the important values we want to live by: family, love, friendships, a healthy marriage, children, and solid relationships.

We can do the same thing at church. In our ministry center, we display our Core Values on our walls. We hang pictures of various teams that remind us of the crucial and joyful place of relationships in ministry success. We have framed collages of each staff person, displaying their homes, pets, families and hobbies, to remind us that each person is an individual, with distinct families and unique dreams. These are not merely "employees" or "office staff." They are individuals who each reflect their Savior in distinct and beautiful ways.

We display these totems in such a way as to graciously remind us daily of what is most important. They are the invisible megaphones that silently cultivate our perceptions, day by day, until our culture grows healthy and vibrant.

We evaluate every piece of communication to ensure that it displays our values and that it does not unconsciously undermine them. Wording in bulletins, pictures, layouts—we review everything. But remember: *it is in our culture, not in a program.*

We do not have a department in charge of scrutinizing bulletins and communications. It's in our DNA.

We do not have an assigned performance review committee. It is built into our relationships and weekly debriefing sessions.

We don't have a formalized watchdog committee, searching for grumblers. It's one of our values from 1 Corinthians 10:10, which reminds us that complaints open the door for the enemy—and we'd really rather keep him out. We have to negotiate enough speed bumps as it is!

Since we live to make each other successful, when we see something going awry, we talk immediately and do what we can to help. When a staff person gets a bit defensive, we graciously try to help him or her work through it. We are all learning and we are all growing.

Why do things happen in this way? It's just the culture we live in!

Choose the Oak Over the Squash

> For you have need of endurance, so that when you have done the will of God, you may receive what was promised (Heb. 10:36).

A hurry-up father once came to see the president of a small college on behalf of his son. He wanted to know if he could get his boy through the four-year program any more quickly and into the workaday world. The president of the college leaned forward and spoke slowly to let his words sink in.

"Well, sir, it all depends on what you want to make of your son. If you want an oak tree, it'll be at least seven years. But you can grow squash in just three months."

Transitioning and shifting the culture of a church won't happen overnight. There are no instant solutions. Culture shifting happens over time and demands sensitive leadership and biblical motives.

But it can happen!

A couple of years ago, I visited a 2,500-member church (let's call it "Redeemer") that had decided it wanted to shift gears from a more traditional approach, in which staff members did much of the work, to a team-based approach, in which volunteer leaders equipped their people to do most of the work. I can't say that the transition went without a hitch, nor can I say that it's yet complete.

But I can report that they're glad they did it—and that others have noticed!

Recently, Redeemer completed a search for a key staff member to replace a talented man who had left to do other things. As the selection process wound to a close, the church narrowed the candidates to three finalists. In the several months leading up to that stage, team-based ministry had really taken hold. Both men and women in the church enthusiastically embraced new leadership roles and developed strong, hard-working teams that carried on the bulk of Redeemer's ministry.

Do you know what I found most remarkable? All three of the finalists for the vacant staff position repeatedly mentioned two qualities at Redeemer that they found extremely appealing: the warm and friendly reception they felt from every church group and individual they met (and each finalist had gone through an extensive interview process involving scores of people); and the pervasive presence of effective, team-based ministry. All three said, in one way or another, "You folks don't know how unusual this is. You have something remarkable going on here! I would love to be a part of something like this."

Is it easy to make the transition? No. Does it come quickly? Again, no. But is it worth it?

Do you even need to *ask*?

You'll See

No church is beyond growth. No congregation can resist the moving of God. Like Luke's account of the raising of Lazarus, even *rigor mortis* has to surrender its dead to the power of God's Word!

In the past, God had to let a generation die in order to start afresh. But I see many young Davids and emerging Joshuas among our ranks. Watch for them. Encourage them. Nurture them. They might be right on your team. They have all the necessary potential to lead the way to a new and thrilling era. All they need to flourish is a healthy culture. Give that to them and they will surprise us all.

You watch. You wait. You'll see!

Team Preparation

1. Do you want your church culture to change? Explain.
2. Answer the following questions with as many specifics as you can manage:
   - What about our church do I like?
   - What about our church draws people to it?
   - What aspects of our church look like weeds?
   - What aspects of our church turn off visitors?
3. What are your church's "totems"? Ask yourself the following questions:

- What are we known for?
- Are these the things we *want* to be known for?
- Are these values biblical?
- Will these remain relevant in the next generation?
- Can we dedicate ourselves to unreservedly live out these values?

4. What kind of discussions have you had with your leaders about these totems?

5. What will *not* change at your church, even in the midst of great change?

6. How can you effectively display your "totems" around your church?

7. How can you make sure that you and everyone in your church give this process the time it requires?

Chapter 13

NURTURING THE TEAM

One of the highest of human duties is the duty of encouragement. There is a regulation of the Royal Navy which says: "No officer shall speak discouragingly to another officer in the discharge of his duties."

WILLIAM BARCLAY, SCOTTISH THEOLOGIAN, 1907–1978

Over my first several years in church ministry, I made an alarming discovery that I never expected to make. I noticed that my strengths also harbored my greatest weaknesses. I learned the hard way that our strongest allies in ministry, if left unguarded, can give cover and support to our worst enemies.

Let me give you one example. While I always enjoyed a lot of success in recruiting new leaders, I also had a hard time in keeping them. Those who climbed on board arrived full of energy, enthusiasm and potential; but not long afterwards, they all jumped from the train, tired and empty and discouraged. Why?

What was happening? I just couldn't figure it out.

It took me a long time to learn from my mistakes, and I paid a high price for the privilege of discovery. After several years of purchasing costly lessons at the expense of a dozen or so wonderfully gifted leaders, I finally determined that there just *had* to be a better way. At last I reached a point where I had picked up a lot of hard-earned wisdom—but by then I had also lost all of my leaders!

Can you guess my problem? While I excelled at recruiting new leaders (a strength), I bombed at nurturing them (a weakness within my strength).

Since I don't want you to shell out for the same expensive lessons I had to buy at the cost of blood, sweat and tears, allow me to offer five principles for nurturing your team.

Incubate the Right Culture

I thank my God in all my remembrance of you, always offering prayer with joy in my every prayer for you (Phil. 1:3-4).

I have three children. Over the years I have watched them grow in height as well as in maturity. One obvious thing I have noticed about growth: You don't have to force it or plead with it to happen. It occurs on its own. If the kids live in a healthy atmosphere and get nutritious food—barring any life-threatening disease or accident—they grow naturally. It's when growth stops despite a healthy environment that I get worried!

God designed churches to be greenhouses for budding leaders and their exciting dreams. Creating an atmosphere of health is one of the simplest, yet most overlooked, factors in growing healthy people and healthy leaders.

If you want to nurture your team, you have to develop the right culture. Within a healthy culture, growing things have a much better chance of becoming fruitful. The latest program or the trendiest conference will never change churches; only the right culture can do that, a healthy environment that powerfully attracts outsiders. Remember that the church is a living organism, not a machine or a mere corporation. Living things are wired for growth and fruitfulness, and the culture that surrounds a church will either stifle that life or encourage it.

What kind of culture exists in your church, among your team?

Some churches develop a culture of fear by the way their leaders react to errors and whether other leaders tolerate or correct such hurtful reactions. A culture like this silently demands performance over grace.

Other churches build a culture of shallow faith or a culture of strict legalism by virtue of what they permit and give silent consent to.

Even an acceptable culture can mutate into a culture of distrust, simply because its leaders start to tolerate unresolved conflicts.

Here's the point: Over time, the way leaders communicate their values builds a certain culture.

Some years ago, my wife and I decided to see the Grand Ole Opry in Nashville, Tennessee, the epicenter of country music. And since we were traveling that far, we reasoned, why stop short of the whole enchilada? So we decided to stay at the Grand Ole Opry Hotel, a sprawling complex that has to be seen to be believed.

Have you ever seen 15 acres of hotel under one roof? That's the Grand Ole Opry Hotel. Outside, Tennessee's midsummer heat could wilt the toughest cowboy—but inside the

Grand Ole Opry Hotel, the climate reminded me of Hawaii. Its air-conditioned, humidity-controlled atmosphere made it most pleasant and inviting. Inside the hotel we even found the flora of Polynesia, in stark contrast to the desert barrenness outside. What would have died outside was thriving inside. What could not grow in the outdoor Nashville bore luxurious fruit in the inside Nashville. And all it took was the right atmosphere!

I remember turning to my wife, Anna, and exclaiming, "This is like the church *should* be! [She always takes the brunt of my spontaneous revelations.] We must develop such a culture of health that those who are dying outside will thrive on the inside!"

We looked at this principle in the last chapter, but at this juncture, I'd like you to stop and ask yourself the following questions about your church:

- What kind of culture do we possess?
- If someone visited us for a week and simply observed, what would they conclude about our team?
- What kind of atmosphere do we have?
- How would outsiders define our spirit or the tone of our environment?
- Do our people work well with one another?
- Do we listen to each other?
- Does everyone demonstrate a high level of respect for one another, including top leaders for others?
- Are we genuinely excited to see one another?

Without building the right culture, even the healthiest plants begin to wilt. If you want to begin nurturing your team in a new way, this is the place to start.

Raise the Value of Healthy Relationships

Did you know that you have a built-in emotional barometer? We all do. I often take a reading of mine to check my level of frustration—is it sunny, partly cloudy, stormy, or somewhere in-between?

Many leaders live with a low-grade discouragement concerning their ministries and personal relationships. A relational failure or encounter that went sour will drop the barometric reading over time. You can't live with that, and neither can I. Remember, it isn't sin that kills God's people; it's *unresolved* sin!

Ministry ought to be fun. It should charge us up. Each time someone comes to see me, the encounter ought to get my motor running and excite my spirit. If it doesn't, I need to do some immediate recalibration.

Some years ago, between speaking engagements at a conference, a man sat down with me and identified himself as a new pastor in town.

"Give me something to energize my church," he pleaded. "We've flatlined for a year and I need something to ignite the spark again. Give me a new program I can start, a talk, a video, *anything!*"

I caught his obvious desperation but pulled back on the reins to slow him down. I thought I smelled a dream killer. I questioned him and discovered that he'd been there only a year.

"So how's it going?" I asked.

"Well," he said with a more thoughtful pace, "it didn't start out very well."

"Tell me about it," I said, hoping to buy a little time so that I could figure out something that might help him.

"The day I took over, the ship was in some rough waters," he replied. "I was the assistant pastor at the time. One Sunday morning the former pastor got up in the pulpit. He asked the board members to stand, and when they did, he said to the whole congregation, 'It's because of these people that I am leaving the church.' He promptly picked up his Bible and left!"

The story stunned me. "No way!" I said. "That didn't happen that morning."

"Oh yes it did!" the young pastor countered. "I was *there*."

"No, it didn't happen that morning," I repeated. "It actually happened a year or two before when the church leadership chose to tolerate broken and unhealthy relationships. Things unresolved went underground, personality conflicts took root and the whole mess culminated on that Sunday morning. It started long before that fateful morning, but nobody seemed to notice. And I have just the program that will remedy that."

He sat on the edge of his seat, ready for my prescription.

"For the next six months," I said, "institute *no new programs*. Instead, make it your goal—and every leader's goal in the church—to ensure that you have healthy relationships with every single person in the church. No new ventures, no new ideas. Condition the soil first, otherwise no plant will survive in this garden of parched, broken ground."

"Well how would *you* start?" he asked.

"Just start by going to every person, looking each one in the eye, and asking, 'Are we OK?' That would be a good beginning. Restore the primacy of healthy relationships, because when you have great relationships, ANY program will fly. Conversely, if you have broken and wounded relationships—if some things have gone underground—then even the best programs you try to start won't bring you success. I assure you they will be sabotaged from within!"

He got very quiet, trying hard to take in such an unexpected strategy. Then I continued: "And try your best to get this program going by Sunday! If not, you might consider canceling church so you can concentrate on restoring healthy relationships."

His eyes widened, then narrowed. "What do you mean? Cancel *church*? Are you crazy? Where did you get that lame idea?"

"Oh, I apologize if I led you to believe that I came up with that idea," I confessed. "I got that out of a book about building great ministries. A guy named Matthew quoted a guy named Jesus. He wrote, 'If therefore you are presenting your offering at the altar, and there remember that your brother has something against you, leave your offering there before the altar, and go your way; first be reconciled to your brother, and then come and present your offering' (Matt. 5: 23-24)."

To make sure he got it, I then offered my own paraphrase: "Turning to His disciples, He simplified truth into everyday language: 'Maintaining healthy relationships is more important than just attending church!'"

In fact, merely attending church while tolerating bad relationships at home usually does more harm than good. It is said that the darkest place of a lighthouse is at its base.

The presence of healthy connections and genuine friendships within the church opens the door to receptivity and acceptance from those outside the church. Most new people can quickly detect the presence of broken, unresolved relationships. Even though we push things underground, you can still smell the odor of death; it's like an open sewer running just beneath the pews. A few minutes after arriving, many newcomers catch the scent of something distinctly unpleasant and unhealthy.

"What a friendly place, but *phew* . . . what is that smell? I don't know where it's coming from, but it's *rancid*!"

We have no choice but to maintain healthy relationships among team members. A healthy atmosphere draws people who crave health. People naturally look for "friendly churches," for places where they can find a few genuine friends. Let's be that kind of church.

Live to Make Others Successful

Rejoice with those who rejoice, and weep with those who weep. Be of the same mind toward one another (Rom. 12:15-16).

In doing church as a team, leaders live to make other team members successful. Not vice versa!

If each member of the team feels cared for and fulfilled, then the whole ministry benefits. If they succeed, then the whole church gets help. Each leader must cultivate a selfless spirit without a gaping need for credit. We release the sweet aroma of life when we live for one another rather than for ourselves. I think that is exactly what Jesus meant when He said that whoever wishes to save his life will lose it (see Matt. 16:25).

It's this principle that makes possible the efficient operation of the human body. My lungs cheer for a healthy heart. Why? Not for the heart's sake alone, but also for the lungs' sake. If the heart goes down, so do the lungs. My stomach cheers on my kidneys. It wants the liver to remain in top form, not only for the kidney's benefit, but also for its own.

As a pastor, I need everyone in my congregation to function well—not for their sake alone but for my health as well. Think about it. If the setup crew doesn't show up come Sunday morning, I am in big trouble! If the worship team drops out or can't get along because of some lingering internal struggles, it affects everything else in the Sunday services. What if the children's ministry falters? It throws everything else off kilter.

Health gives birth to health, and disease leads to more disease. Which do you want on your team? It really is a choice.

> *We release the sweet aroma of life when we live for one another rather than for ourselves.*

If the four on my fractal team succeed, then so do I. If they fail or stumble, then so do I. If they hurt, I hurt. When they rejoice, I rejoice. When they fire on all cylinders, I can see the congregation zooming down the highway in a nifty red convertible, laughing, and getting to where they want to be. I feel a fresh breeze blowing and gulp in the delightful scent of vibrancy and excitement—and it thrills my soul. But if they feel discouraged or overloaded with unresolved struggles, in no time at all I see the congregation bumping along in an old jalopy, their faces covered in gloom and breathing in the noxious fumes of a jammed-up highway made worse by a windless, humid day.

We live to make each other successful! Let's take a lesson from our bodies.

Stewarding Authority

For this reason I am writing these things while absent, in order that when present I may not use severity, in accordance with the authority which the Lord gave me, *for building up and not for tearing down* (2 Cor. 13:10, emphasis added).

Paul well explains the purpose for authority in the church. God intends it to build people up, not tear them down. Accepting and practicing this single truth will transform your people skills.

God has no problem giving us authority when we use it for His purpose—to build people up. The gift of authority puts you in a position to encourage others and to bring out the best in people, so don't use it as a tool to leverage people in order to fulfill your own desires.

When I was just starting in Bible college, the president asked me to sing at one of our denomination's conventions. Being a novice as well as a young Christian, it took all I had just to stand in front of this dignified group of pastors and leaders. I felt so nervous that, as my time to sing approached, all the water drained out of my mouth and into my hands.

In my BC days, this would have been a cakewalk. I've played with rock and roll bands with hundreds prancing on the dance floor—with one major exception. Usually, most in the audience were drunk and/or stoned. They had only requirement of the band: each rendition had to feature a loud and nauseating beat, something that the bass guitarist and drummer felt only too happy to deliver.

The convention was held in one of our denomination's oldest and most distinguished churches. Just before the main speaker came to podium, I got introduced as a new Bible college student who had recently given his heart to the Lord. I was to give a short testimony and then sing an original song.

Standing before 700 pastors, I noticed something strangely different from my BC days. This audience looked both still and listening! I wasn't used to this, and so far as I could see, none of them appeared stoned.

Nerves stripped my song down to the bare minimum and flattened all the high notes. My mind went blank on the second verse, so I made up another one on the fly. It was horrible. I prayed secretly that the Lord would come and rapture me out of there before the song ended.

Finally, the ordeal came to a merciful close. The Amish-looking group mustered up a brief courtesy clap, and I quickly found my seat. Sitting in a puddle of perspiration, I made a secret vow that as soon as the main speaker closed, I would grab my guitar and flee—not just the conference, but from Bible college. I thought that if I couldn't stand before convinced Christians, how would I ever stand before non-Christians? I felt so inadequate and phony.

The speaker concluded, and I lunged for my guitar. But when I did, I felt a strong hand on my shoulder. I spun around and found myself face-to-face with the renowned pastor of the grand church in which I stood. He looked straight through me and motioned me to sit back down.

Thoughts of despair ran through my mind. I was history! I just knew I was about to be expelled or, I hoped, mercifully reprimanded. I braced myself for the worst.

He looked deeply at me for a moment and then began. Because of his authority and my deep respect for him, his words indelibly etched themselves into my soul.

"Wayne," he said, "I observed a great victory tonight."

"Really?" I pressed. "Where?"

Without answering my question, he continued. "You were nervous tonight, weren't you?" I didn't tell him that I had made up the whole second verse.

He continued, "I want you to know how impressed I was by

your sincerity. I watched you win a decisive battle tonight. You could have bolted. You could have just stopped and walked off the platform. But you didn't. You want to know why?"

By this time, I felt desperate, and blurted out, "Why? Tell me, please!"

"Because you love Jesus more than man's applause."

I felt stunned.

"You see," he continued, "sometimes I want to quit. I make a mistake and I beat myself to death because of it. But from now on, when I want to quit, I will remember a young Bible college student who refused to do so, and I will draw strength from that. Remember, Wayne, courage isn't the absence of fear; it is pressing on in spite of it. Keep singing. Keep speaking to people of His great love. His hand will be on you."

I am in ministry today probably because one man stewarded his authority well. He could have flattened my spirit with a well-deserved rebuke, but he used his authority to repair my sagging heart instead.

God would love to restore authority to His church, but only under one condition: That we steward it for the purposes for which He gives it, to build others up and not destroy them.

Do you want more authority? Then start building people up! It's just that simple. When God sees that you are willing to use whatever authority you have to encourage the best in others, He will give you more. I pray that our churches will be filled with great authority, as we see God's people realizing their dreams and becoming all they can be for the King.

Watch Your Starting Points

Do you want to nurture your team? Then don't start at *your* starting point; start at *theirs*.

In the early years, I tended to think, *Why can't these volunteers do it right? I can do it with my eyes closed!*

I'm so glad Jesus didn't think that way. I rejoice that He didn't look out over the whitened banisters of heaven, thinking, *Why can't those earthlings get it together! I can't believe how human they are!* No. Instead, the Scriptures comfort us by exclaiming, "For God so loved the world that He gave His only begotten Son." God did not start by forcing us into His grid of understanding; instead, His love compelled Him to venture into ours.

Start by telling yourself that regardless of the outcome, everyone really is trying their best. Sure, there will be foibles and fumbles, but everyone is trying their best. A first grader may finish far behind an elite sprinter, but the slower time does not necessarily equate to a lazy, uncaring runner. Each person has reached different levels of character, competency, and maturity, and the real reason God had that person hook up with you may have nothing to do with the task at hand. Maybe He wants you to help them grow past their immaturities, rather than disqualify them for it.

In my book *The Dream Releasers*, I tell the story of a softball game that became a divine classroom for me. I'd like to retell it here.

Having grown up with a father who served as a First Sergeant in the U.S. Army, in my earlier years I had a tendency to be fairly hard on people. I did surgery without anesthesia and I used an axe where a scalpel might have been more appropriate. I thought my gift was to be a hammer, and when you think that, everybody else is a nail.

I remember the afternoon when God showed up at our church softball game. We had made it to the finals, so this would be an important match. I was a coach-player and assigned each of my players to his position. Our left fielder was a young college student named John. He usually played very skillfully, but today would be an exception.

The first batter to the plate hit a long line drive to John, who got caught flat-footed as he watched the ball sail over his head for a home run.

"Shake it off, John. Now let's buckle down!" I shouted from the dugout. I was trying to sound like an authentic coach, but in reality I wanted to scream.

On the next play our third baseman mishandled a grounder and it trailed into the outfield. John grabbed the wayward ball and heaved it so far over the first baseman's head that it sailed over the opposing dugout and into the spectators.

I didn't feel ready this time to tell John to shake it off, because I really wanted to shake his neck! After all, these were the finals, and such terrible errors just couldn't be tolerated.

I called for a time-out and pulled John from the field. I told him that it was too important of a game for such remedial mistakes, and that I personally would go out to left field. "We have to stop this kind of bleeding," I told him as I jogged into position.

Whether someone told the hitters to key in on left field, I will never know, but the next several hits all rocketed toward my coordinates. The first one sailed so far over my head that it looked like Halley's comet. Two batters later, a screaming line drive flew by me so fast that I hardly had time to get out of its way. (I could have made the catch if our pitcher hadn't thrown such a fast pitch.) But the final straw? A high pop fly hit me in the chest. (I lost it in the sun.)

Completely humiliated, I could see John in the dugout with his head buried in his hands. He's never disclosed to me whether he was crying or laughing hysterically, because from a distance, they look the same.

That's when God showed up. As I rehearsed the excuses I'd

use at the end of the inning, God spoke.

"Were you trying your best?"

"Absolutely," I replied.

"And so was John. Everybody out here is trying his best. Never forget that."

We didn't have a long conversation that day, but I will never forget the lesson. Everyone is trying their best with as much as they know how. Granted, we may have to deal with some immaturity and undeveloped character—but everyone is doing the best they can.

Wanted: Gentle Restorers

Can you hear it? God is issuing a call for gentle restorers, with an emphasis on both words.

Churches and families don't need self-appointed watchdogs who attack their own family members. We need Dream Releasers who understand the heart of God and who long to impart the same to sprained ankles and bruised hearts.

> If someone falls into sin, forgivingly restore him, saving your critical comments for yourself. You might be needing forgiveness before the day's out (Galatians 6:1, *THE MESSAGE*).

That gets me right where I live. And while I can't be too sure about this—I wouldn't want you to hold me to it—but I wonder if, just maybe, God added this verse to the Bible after my softball game.

For sure, I didn't see it clearly before then. Probably lost it in the sun. But what a difference it makes when the Son opens your eyes.

May He do the same for you.

Team Preparation

1. What kind of culture do we have in our church? Is it healthy or unhealthy?
2. In what areas can we improve immediately?
3. Take a few minutes to write a note to your pastor and team members to let them know of your support. If you are a pastor, take time right now to send a note of appreciation to your key leaders, thanking them for partnering with you in doing church as a team. This kind of exercise is what builds healthy environments where leaders get nurtured, not just used.

A MOVING PICTURE

Some time ago, I went to see a movie featuring a magnificent story line. During my two hours in the dark theater, I watched a tapestry of people and events spin before my eyes. What a wonderful experience!

On the way out—being the curious sort of person who loves to see how things work—I walked up a short flight of stairs and poked my nose into the projection booth. The film that had just thrilled my heart sat spooled on a large, round platter. There must have been a mile or two of film, with each frame holding a tiny portion of the story.

The light rays of the projector had cast a beam onto the screen while frame after frame rolled steadily before it—frame after frame after frame. The quick but steady pace of the advancing frames gave the images the illusion of moving; hence, the original name of the "moving picture" shows, as they were called during my grandfather's days.

Suppose you stopped one of the frames and held it still before the projector lens? You would see an image in suspended animation (just before the film melted from the intense heat of the xenon lamp). Seeing that one frame alone, without the rest of the frames marching in cadence, wouldn't give you much understanding of the movie. To understand the whole story, you need that one frame moving in sequence with its many thousands of brothers.

Every one of us is like a single frame in God's story, and each frame is incredibly important to God's plan. How often we think that no one would miss us if we didn't show up! But if a bunch of frames decided to go on strike and walk out of the film, how would we make any sense of the movie?

Unfortunately, we sometimes do just that as Christians. Justifying our inaction by our tiny, insignificant existence, we choose not to get involved. And when that happens, no wonder the world gets such a jumpy and jerky picture of the church!

If we are serious about presenting a clear picture of the Lord to a desperate world, then we must each take our place. Be faithful in the frame that God has allotted to your care! Develop it with color. Then plug into the cadence of those with whom He has called you into service.

And as we do church as a team,[1] you'll see one of the most beautiful and moving pictures of the heart of Jesus unfold right before your eyes.

Ho`omakaukau? I mua!

Ready? Paddle forward!

Note

1. You need to know that I have so much yet to learn. I am still writing this book. As time goes on, I plan to add to it. Often I feel as if I am in the kindergarten stage of learning how to shepherd God's people and how to build leaders who will catch the heart and vision of Jesus Christ for the lost.

    Even so, I love what I see God beginning to do in the churches. A new wine is being poured out, and only hearts made of new wineskins will be able to survive the pour. The others will burst and spill their contents, remaining ornate but empty.

    This world is crying out for godly leaders who will allow the Holy Spirit to develop within them a spirit of excellence and an ongoing desire to receive advice and remain teachable. I want to be one of those leaders. Will you join me?

ABOUT THE AUTHOR

Wayne Cordeiro is senior pastor of New Hope Christian Fellowship in Oahu, a work planted in September 1995. Within 9 years, attendance at weekend services had grown to 10,500, and it had planted 22 churches in Hawaii. More than 26,000 people received Christ for the first time during these first years of the church.

Under New Hope, 67 churches have been birthed in Hawaii, Africa, Australia, Philippines, Myanmar, Japan and parts of the mainland United States. Prior to moving to Oahu, Wayne was senior pastor at New Hope Christian Fellowship in Hilo, Hawaii, for almost 12 years.

Wayne grew up in the Palolo Valley on Oahu. He lived in Japan for three years, then moved to Oregon where he finished his schooling at Eugene Bible College. He served with Youth For Christ for seven years and as a staff pastor for three years at Faith Center Foursquare Church in Eugene, Oregon, before returning to Hawaii.

He is an accomplished songwriter who has released six albums. His "Words of New Hope," a radio broadcast, airs daily in Hawaii as well as in Oregon. In addition, New Hope's services are televised throughout Hawaii. As president of the Pacific Rim Bible College, Wayne is working to train, develop and support emerging leaders who will plant twenty-first-century churches around the Pacific Rim.

Wayne travels extensively throughout the islands, the continental United States and Asia to speak at conferences, churches, civic gatherings, prisons, business forums and leadership conventions. He also speaks to companies and corporations about restructuring and growth strategies.

He has written eight books: *Doing Church as a Team, Attitudes That Attract Success, Gems Along the Way, The Dream Releasers, Indispensable Life Lessons, Culture Shift, Rising Above* and the forthcoming Regal book, *The Divine Mentor.*

Pastor Wayne and his wife, Anna, have three children, Amy, Aaron and Abigail, all of whom serve with him in ministry.

Further information about resources may be found on the website: http://www.enewhope.org.